Euripides

The Trojan Women

ΤΩΝ 51	ΛΙΤΣΟΥ ΑΣΗΜΩ ΙΩ.	ΕΤΩΝ 63
» 19	ΛΟΥΚΑΣ ΓΕΩΡΓΙΟΣ ΕΥΣΤ.	» 62
» 26	ΛΟΥΚΑ ΠΑΝΩΡΑΙΑ ΓΕΩΡ.	» 41
» 19	ΛΟΥΚΑ ΧΡΥΣΟΥΛΑ ΑΝΑΣΤ.	» 23
» 78	ΛΟΥΚΑΣ ΙΩΑΝΝΗΣ ΑΝΑΣΤ.	» 2
» 76	ΛΟΥΚΑ ΑΡΤΕΜΗΣΙΑ ΑΝΑΣΤ.	» 85
» 59	ΛΑΓΟΣ ΓΕΩΡΓΙΟΣ ΚΩΝ. ●	» 31
» 38	ΜΑΛΑΜΟΣ ΣΠΥΡΙΔΩΝ ΑΝΑΣΤ.	» 67
» 12	ΜΑΛΑΜΟΥ ΛΟΥΚΙΑ ΣΠΥΡ.	» 8
» 6	ΜΑΛΑΜΟΥ ΔΗΜΗΤΡΑ ΑΝΑΣΤ.	» 38
» 5	ΜΑΛΑΜΟΣ ΙΩΑΝΝΗΣ ΑΝΑΣΤ.	» 9
» 3	ΜΑΡΙΟΣ ΠΑΝΑΓΙΩΤΗΣ ΔΗΜΟΥ	» 68
» 44	ΜΑΡΙΟΥ ΠΑΝΩΡΑΙΑ ΔΗΜ.	» 41
» 34	ΜΑΣΤΟΓΙΑΝΝΗΣ ΝΙΚΟΛ. ΛΟΥΚ.	» 71
» 39	ΜΑΣΤΟΓΙΑΝΝΗ ΕΛΙΣΑΒ. ΛΟΥΚ.	» 29
» 32	ΜΙΧΑΣ ΓΕΩΡΓΙΟΣ ΝΙΚΟΛ.	» 60
» 63	ΜΙΧΑΣ ΗΡΑΚΛΗΣ ΙΩ.	» 66
» 19	ΜΠΑΛΑΓΟΥΡΑΣ ΝΙΚΟΛΑΟΣ ΙΩ.	» 49
» 39	ΜΠΑΛΑΓΟΥΡΑ ΘΕΟΧΟΥ ΠΑΝ.	» 71
» 33	ΜΠΑΜΠΑΝΟΠΟΥΛΟΥ ΧΡΥΣ. Β.	» 46
» 29	ΜΠΑΜΠΑΝΟΠΟΥΛΟΥ ΣΟΦ. Β.	» 6
» 52	ΜΠΑΡΛΟΥ ΤΑΣΙΑ ΧΡΙΣΤΟΦ.	» 44
» 68	ΜΠΑΡΛΟΥ●ΛΟΥΚΙΑ ΠΑΝ.	» 29
» 33	ΜΠΑΡΛΟΥ ΤΑΣΟΥΛΑ ΠΑΝ.	» 4
» 22	ΜΠΑΡΛΟΥ ΑΒΑΠΤΙΣΤΟΝ ΠΑΝ. 5 ΜΗΝ.
» 76	ΜΠΑΡΛΟΥ ΕΛΕΝΗ ΛΟΥΚ.	ΕΤΩΝ 9
» 23	ΜΠΑΣΔΕΚΗ ΓΑΡΥΦΑΛ. ΑΝΑΣΤ.	» 32
» 5	ΜΠΑΣΔΕΚΗ ΕΛΕΝΗ ΑΝΑΣΤ.	» ?
» 1	ΜΠΑΣΔΕΚΗ ΑΝΘΟΥΛΑ ΕΥΘ.	» 80

Euripides

The Trojan Women

Translation, Introduction, Notes, and Appendices
Diskin Clay
DUKE UNIVERSITY

focus an imprint of
Hackett Publishing Company, Inc.
Indianapolis/Cambridge

For my three daughters,

ταῖς χάρισιν,

Andreia

Hilary

Christine

Euripides: The Trojan Women
© 2005 Diskin Clay

Previously published by Focus Publishing/R. Pullins Company

Focus an imprint of
Hackett Publishing Company, Inc.
P.O. Box 44937
Indianapolis, Indiana 46244-0937

www.hackettpublishing.com

For information regarding performance rights, please email us at
Permissions@hackettpublishing·com

Cover: Mourning Women. The Memorial at Distomo, Phokis. Photo by author.

ISBN 13: 978-1-58510-111-5

26 25 24 23   7 8 9 10

Table of Contents

Illustrations

Introduction

> He grew old among the flames of Troy
> and the quarries of Sicily.
> —George Seferis, *Euripides The Athenian*

1 The Flames of Troy: Euripides and the Aftermath of the Iliad

The Trojan Women is a play on the consequences of war and the fate of those defeated in war and the fate of their victors. Like Aeschylus' *Persians*, it is presented from the point of view of the conquered. It was written in the middle of the Peloponnesian War (431-405) and produced in the competitions of the festival of Dionysos in spring of 415, just months before the Athenians launched their great armada against Syracuse and Sicily. If *The Trojan Women* is a war play, it is not about a specific war; it is about all wars.

The title of the play is *Troades, The Trojan Women*. It centers on the Trojan women taken captive during the sack of Troy in the tenth year of the Trojan War. One of the captive Trojan women, Polyxena, was murdered before the opening of Euripides' play. The rest are about to be dispersed as slaves throughout the Greek world, and the son of Hector will be murdered by the victorious Greek army. Yet Euripides' *Trojan Women* survives in the dramatic literature and opera of Europe and even in the musical setting for soprano voice of Hecuba's lament by Gustav Holtz. We are reminded by Gilbert Murray's version of the play at the beginning of World War I (1915) and the version Jean-Paul Sartre produced during the Algerian War (*Les Troyennes*, 1965) that Euripides' *Trojan Women* revives in the crisis of war and is endlessly adaptable.

Euripides might have been born in 480, the year of the defeat of the Persian fleet off the island of Salamis, an island that he seems to have been peculiarly attached to. (There are two references to it in *The Trojan Women*.) There is a tradition that he composed his tragedies in the isolation of a cave on the island. But Seferis was right in his *Euripides the Athenian*: Euripides grew old in the light of the flames of Troy and the darkness of the quarries of Syracuse, where the remnants of the Athenian expeditionary force were imprisoned in 413. A tradition has it that some Athenian prisoners awaiting death were freed because they could sing for the Syracusans arias from the plays of Euripides. It has been suggested that the lyrics of *The Trojan Women* were much appreciated in Syracuse and saved some Athenian lives.[1]

The immediate setting of Euripides' *Trojan Women* was the major dramatic festival of the spring of 415, when Euripides was 65. In late March and the Attic month of Elaphebolion, the sea became, as the proverb went, navigable. Visitors from the subject states of the Delian league could cross the Aegean to witness this festival held to honor Dionysos and to magnify the state of Athens. As a part of this long seven-day festival, Athenians (women included) and visitors to Athens gathered in the theater of Dionysos where they could admire the tribute of the "allied" city-states, as this was carried into the orchestra of the theater and displayed, even before the actors and chorus of the first tragedy had made their entry. The audience could also view the procession of the orphaned children of Athenians who had fallen in battle.[2]

There are more remote settings to *The Trojan Women*. They frame the *Iliad*. These are the traditions on the periphery of the *Iliad* that provide the history of Troy in the generation before Priam. Euripides knew these traditions and expected that his audience would recognize them in the background of his play. Before the first Greek assault on Troy, there was an earlier assault by Herakles, Philoctetes, and Telamon. In Trojan history there was the legend of Hecuba's dream that she had given birth to a torch; alarmed by the portent, she and Priam exposed the infant Alexandros. He was saved from exposure by a herdsman and, as a young herdsman, Paris made a fateful choice of one of three goddesses who presented themselves to him in a contest of beauty. These traditions are barely recognized in Homer's *Iliad* (cf. 24.23-30), but the traditions concerning what happened in Troy before the wrath of Achilles were set out in the first play of what is sometimes called Euripides' "Trojan Trilogy," the *Alexandros*. The second play of this "trilogy" is the *Palamedes* (a hero not mentioned by

1   The tradition that Athenians who could sing lyric passages from Euripides were spared by the victorious Syracusans is attested in Plutarch, *Nicias* 29.2-3. That they chose to sing arias from *The Trojan Women* is the congenial conjecture of Léon Parmentier, *Euripide, Les Troyennes* (Paris 1959) 25.

2   Simon Goldhill has written an important study of the ceremonies surrounding the production of Athenian tragedy and the "ideology" of the major festival of Dionysos in Athens, "The Great Dionysia and Civic Ideology," in John J. Winkler and Froma I. Zeitlin, eds., *Nothing to Do with Dionysos?* (Princeton 1990) 97-129.

Homer). It too takes place before the opening of the *Iliad*. The last play of this unique Euripidean "trilogy" is *The Trojan Women*. It takes place after the fall of Troy and the burial of Hector, "the tamer of horses" (as he is described in the last line of the *Iliad*). The satyr play performed last and making a tetralogy of a trilogy was the *Sisyphos*.

The story Homer did not tell is supplied by the short post-Homeric epics known in antiquity as The Epic Cycle. Three of these epics concern us most directly, as they concerned Euripides: the so-called *Cypria*, where the Judgment of Paris is described, the *Little Iliad*, and *The Sack of Troy* (*Iliupersis*). These events were also depicted in vase painting. Euripides dramatized the subjects of these minor epics to provide a history both of the causes of the Trojan War and the fall of Troy that follows on the death of Hector. It is not a continuous history, as is, for example the one surviving trilogy, Aeschylus' *Oresteia*.

The final episode in *The Trojan Women* is one that justifies Euripides' title as the "most tragic" of tragedians: this is the last scene in which Hecuba bends over the body of her grandson, Astyanax, and laments his death. In *The Little Iliad*, the murder of Hector and Andromache's son Astyanax is described. In this version, it is Achilles' son, Pyrrhos, who takes the infant from his nurse and throws him down from the one of the towers of Troy. This report helps us appreciate Euripides' choice of Odysseus as the Greek responsible for the murder of Astyanax.[3] As we shall see, Odysseus plays a villain's role in the *Palamedes* as well as in *The Trojan Women*. Another source for the incidents immediately following the death of Hector is *The Fall of Troy* by Arktinos of Miletos. The theme is often depicted on Attic vases.

There is a unique scene from the *Iliad* that looks grimly forward to the fate of the Trojan women. It clearly impressed Euripides. This is the narrative in *Iliad* 6 of Hector's return to Troy for a last time. Here Homer describes his meeting with his mother Hecuba and the supplication of the cult statue of Athena on the Trojan acropolis by Hecuba and the women of Troy. Then follows the scene of Hector's last meeting with his wife Andromache and his last moments with his infant son Astyanax, who is frightened by the nodding plume on his father's helmet (236-501). The indifference of the gods of "sacred Ilion" (in this play Zeus, Poseidon, and Athena) to their votaries and the rejection of the rich gift of a cloak draped on the knees of the goddess Athena (addressed by her priestess as "Savior of the City," *Iliad* 6.305) is evoked in the last choral ode of the play.

---

3   This is T 20 Malcolm Davies' *Epicorum Graecorum Fragmenta*, Göttingen 1988. The Epic Cycle is conveniently presented by Davies in *The Greek Epic Cycle*, second edition, London 2001. The evidence for the poems of the Cycle is set out here in pp. 1-12.

Figure 1: Captive Andromache *by Frederic Leighton (1886–88).*
Manchester Art Gallery. PD-ART. Wikimedia.

Hector's last words to his wife are recalled in the Prologue as the
chorus contemplate their fate as slaves in Greece. Hector's words were
prophetic, and Euripides listened closely to his prophecy (*Iliad* 6.448-
63 in my translation):

> The day will come when the sacred city of Troy will fall
> and Priam and the people of Priam of the strong ash
>   spear.
> But in this future I am not as pained for the Trojans
> or for Hecuba herself or for Lord Priam
> or for my brothers who will fall bravely in great
>   numbers in the dust
> under the spear and sword of enemy warriors as I am
>   pained for you.
> Some Achaean in a bronze tunic
> will lead you away with him, and you will weep as he
>   takes from you your day of freedom.
> In Argos you will weave at a loom for a new mistress;
> you will carry water from the springs of Messeis and
>   Hyperie
> and suffer still other disgraces. Strong Necessity will lie
>   upon you.
> And the man who sees you in tears will say of you:
> "This is the wife of Hector, who was once the greatest
>   warrior
> of the Trojans who break horses when they fought
>   around Ilion."

Euripides' appreciation of this scene from the *Iliad* is manifest not only in the Parodos of the *Trojan Women*, where the captive women wonder to what part of Greece they will be taken and from which springs they will be forced to draw water as slaves, but in the scene that introduces Andromache in the *Andromache* carrying a golden vessel from a spring (166-67).

2 The Quarries of Sicily: Athens 415-413

In the *Iliad*, Hector named two springs, Messeis and Hyperie; there is now no certainty as to where they are to be located. By contrast, the geography of *The Trojan Women* is both precise and significantly anachronistic. Anachronism in Euripides is not a symptom of ineptitude. It is the poet's way of making the events of Troy contemporary and relevant to his audience in the theater of Dionysos. In the Parodos, the chorus of Trojan women mention a spring, Peirene (205-6). Peirene is a spring in Corinth (mentioned in *Medea* 69 and Pindar, *Olympian* 13.61), but unnoticed in Homer. They mention Athens. Athens is a place that barely stood on the far horizon of the *Iliad*. Yet for Euripides' Trojan women it is the "renowned" and "blessed" land of Theseus (208-9). As for the "land of Theseus", Theseus was so marginal to Homer that attempts to associate him and Athens with the Trojan War provoked the proverb "nothing without Theseus" (Plutarch, *Theseus* 28.3). Thessaly (214), the second wishful choice of the chorus, is a natural choice, for Achilles' home, Phthia, was a part of Thessaly. But Sicily, a land the chorus mention after Athens (220), is unnamed in the Homeric poems. It is the object of the Athenian expedition that was to leave Athens three months after the production of *The Trojan Women*. Last named is the River Krathis on the Ionian Sea (224-39); it flows by a colony founded under Athenian leadership in 444/443 after the destruction of Sybaris, as the Athenians moved a long step closer to Sicily.

The most striking symptom that in Euripides' *Trojan Women* Troy stands as an emblem for the vanity of victory and conquest is the anachronism that transforms Homeric Greece into Euripides' Greece. The past of Troy is the present of Greece. Euripides represents on stage and in the orchestra the action of a single day after the taking of Troy. But his play wears the face of Janus: it turns us back to the past and forward to the future.

The lyrics of the *Trojan Women* look back (in the first *stasimon*) to the night Troy fell to the stratagem of the Wooden Horse (511-67); in the second *stasimon* the chorus look back on the more distant past of their city and the first expedition launched from Greece against

Troy (799-818). The chorus in its lyrics and Kassandra in her trochaic tetrameters also look forward: Kassandra to her fate, the fate of her captor, Agamemnon, and the fate of Odysseus (427-61); the chorus to their fate as slaves to Greeks (in lines 197-229 of the Parodos).

But the language of the chorus, and occasionally the language of Euripides' actors, looks deeper into the future. An odd, but significant, anachronism occurs in the Prologue. Here Poseidon speaks of the Athenians as having taken their share of captive Trojan women in the Greek lottery that disposed of them (30-31). In the *Iliad*, the Athenians —"the pride of Athens, Theseus' sons"—play a role that rivals that of the Arcadians in its insignificance. Athens was a minor state in the Homeric epic; but in Euripides' *Trojan Women* it is a power to be reckoned with. It figures in the imagination of the Trojan women as the place they would choose, if they could have their choice, for their captivity and slavery: "the renowned, blessed, and prosperous land of Theseus" (208). Significantly, the more distant horizons of the island of Sicily now enter their far reaching thoughts (220-29). Athens remains on their mind. In their evocation of the memory of Ganymede in the second stasimon (820-39), the history of Telamon and the first Greek expedition against Troy evokes the thought of Telamon's island kingdom, Salamis, and Athens on the mainland of Attica opposite. The association is meaningful only in the context of the fifth century.

Athens is described by the chorus in language that is so unmistakably epinician and Pindaric that it now deserves more generous quotation. Pindar wrote victory odes in which both the victor at the panhellenic games and his city were praised. Euripides, who wrote a victory ode for Alcibiades, composed these lines in praise of Athens (799-804):

> O Telamon, King of Salamis, land flowering with bees,
> you established your home and seat
> on an island washed by beating waves
> facing the sacred slope
> where Athena first revealed the sprig of olive, green and
>   gray,
> a celestial crown and jewel for bright, prosperous
>   Athens.

Athens, the brilliant, holy, god-graced city that glimmers on the horizon of the Trojan women's imagination, is not introduced into the scene of the destruction of Troy as an attempt to please the crowd in the theater of Dionysos. As Socrates remarked in Plato's *Menexenus*, it is easy to praise Athens in Athens (236A). In the lyrics of the *The Trojan Women*, Athens seems a privileged place, chosen and protected by divinity, like the Trojan Ganymede of the Salamis ode. But Athena, who displayed her sacred olive on Attic soil in a hierophantic gesture, is, like the other gods, a fickle god, the god who is, as Poseidon describes her, capable of leaping from friendship to hostility (67-68).

Another setting for Euripides' *Trojan Women* is larger than the theater of Dionysos and the Greater Dionysia of 415. It is the theater of the Peloponnesian War, which had entered into its second stage after the "Peace of Nicias" (of 421) was dissolved by Athenian intrigue in the Peloponnesus. In this larger context two events loom large. The first is the brutal treatment of the independent state of Melos in the Cyclades, an island that had attempted to remain outside the bipolarity of power that divided the Greek world into Athenian and Spartan leagues. This came in the summer of 416. The issues involved in Athens' easy conquest of Melos are articulated in the "dialogue" Thucydides composed to illustrate the rhetoric of Athenian power. The power of this rhetoric was grounded on a force of thirty-three ships carrying some 3,000 troops. When the power of words failed, the Athenians turned to force and put to death all Melians of military age and enslaved the women and children (*The Peloponnesian War* 5.84-116). The second event in the theater of the Peloponnesian war lay in the future: the Athenian invasion of the island of Sicily.

Thucydides' narrative continues with the winter of 416 and the Athenian decision to send an expedition against the Dorian states of Sicily. In the syntax of his narrative of the events of the war he gives an indication of his silent judgment of the arrogant confidence of the Athenians. This expedition, launched on a wave of popular enthusiasm, looms in the immediate future of the Greater Dionysia of 415. In a way, it comes as the fulfillment of Kassandra's prophecy in *The Trojan Women* as she speaks of Odysseus' fate after he leaves Troy in ashes (431-40):

> Unhappy man, Odysseus does not know what sufferings
>   await him.
> The day will come when he will look back on my
>   sufferings
> and the sufferings of the Phrygians as a golden age.
> When he has added ten years to the ten years he has
>   spent here, he will arrive at home alone.
> He will come first to the narrow passage between cliffs
> where dread Charybdis dwells. I see the Cyclops,

>   a mountain cannibal. I see Ligurian Circe, who
>   transforms men into pigs.
>   I see shipwrecks on the salt sea, the craving for the lotus,
>   the sacred cattle of the Sun God whose bleeding flesh
>   will one day sing a bitter song that will make Odysseus'
>   flesh crawl.

Euripides could not know the outcome of the Sicilian expedition which was being planned as he entered the tragic competitions in the spring of 415. But Sicily to the west was very much on the horizon of Athenian ambitions. By the time of Thucydides, the Island of the Sun of the *Odyssey* was commonly identified as Sicily. Because of the folly of his hungry men roasting cattle sacred to the Sun (Helios), Odysseus lost those of his companions who had survived that far on their way home to Ithaka (*Odyssey* 12.260-419).[4] Talthybios had warned Kassandra against using the threatening language of prophecy as the Greek army prepared to sail from Troy (408-10), but his warning fell on deaf ears.

There were few voices like that of Kassandra raised in the spring of 415 when the sea—both the Aegean and the Ionian—opened for travel. One motive for travel was *theoria*, the desire to observe the festival of Dionysos in Athens; another was military. In mid-summer, the major part of the expedition to Sicily set out from Athens. The mood in Athens is recorded by Thucydides (*The Peloponnesian War* 6.30-32.2 in my translation):

>   The Athenians and any allies who were in Athens at the time
>   went down to Piraeus at dawn on the day appointed and
>   manned the ships to put out to sea. The rest of the people,
>   in fact, almost the entire population of Athens, citizens and
>   foreigners alike, went down to the Piraeus with them. The
>   natives had people to see off on their way, friends, or relatives,
>   or sons. They came full of hope and full of lamentation at
>   the same time, thinking of the conquests that might be made
>   and thinking, too, of those whom they might never see again,
>   considering the long voyage they were undertaking from
>   their own country. At this moment, when they were on the

---

4   An island called Thrinakie is mentioned in *Odyssey* 11.107. One of the names for
     Sicily (once called Sikania) was Trinakria, the island with three capes. (Coins of
     Syracuse show the emblem of three legs in recognition of this.) The association
     between the island of the Sun, Thrinakie, and Sicily is made by Thucydides in
     The Peloponnesian War 6.2.2.

point of parting from each other to face all the risks ahead, the danger of the situation came home to them more than it had at the time when they voted for the expedition. Nevertheless, they were heartened by the strength they had and the kinds and the quantity of equipment displayed before their eyes. As for the foreigners and the rest of the crowd, they came merely to see the show and to admire the incredible ambition of the thing.

A blast of a trumpet signaled the beginning of the expedition as ships cast off from the Piraeus. In his translation of *The Trojan Women*, Gilbert Murray had a trumpet sound at the end of the play as a signal that the captive women are to be taken to the waiting Greek ships. Clearly, Murray wanted to connect the trumpet blast that signaled the forced departure of the Trojan women from Troy (1266-7) and the trumpet blast of the summer of 415.[5]

Euripides knew that the sub-epic narrative of the destruction of Troy, the *Iliupersis*, was only a half a tale. Beyond this tale lay the *Nostoi* or the returns home, many of which involved the sufferings of the Greek victors, commemorated not only in the *Odyssey* but in dramatic form in Aeschylus' *Oresteia* and Euripides' own *Palamedes*. Beyond the brutal treatment of Melos in the winter of 416/415, which was still a vivid memory when Athens fell to the Spartan admiral, Lysander in 404,[6] lay the great embarkation of the Athenian fleet, the final defeat of the armada and Athenian land forces in 413, and the imprisonment of the survivors in the quarries of Syracuse. Euripides could not have foretold the precise details of the two years of Athenian history that followed the production of his *Trojan Women*. The play won only second place, but, if Euripides was not popular in Athens (a city he left forever in 408), his lyrics were popular in Syracuse.

The thought that humans are not powerful enough to secure their successes from reversal is simply expressed in Euripides' epigram for the Athenians who were lost during the Sicilian expedition:[7]

> These brave men here defeated the men of Syracuse
> in eight battles, when divinity stood equally on each
> side.

---

5   Euripides, *Trojan Women*, London 1915; also *Euripides and his Age* (second edition, Oxford 1946) 87.

6   The scene is powerfully described by Xenophon in his *Hellenika* 2.2.3.

7   Euripides, no. II in Denys Page, *Epigrammata Graeca* (Oxford 1975) p. 44.

The gods did not stand equally by the Athenians to the end, no more than they stood by the Trojans. If Euripides' *Trojan Women* was produced in times of war and in the middle of the grueling Peloponnesian War, it is not about any particular war. It is about war, in which conquerors and conquered are all victims.

3 The "Trojan Trilogy" of 415: *Alexandros, Palamedes, Trojan Women*[8]

All tragedies entered into competition at the festivals of Dionysos in Athens count as "tetralogies." Three tragedies and one satyr play were entered by each of the three competing tragedians. In the case of Aeschylus' *Oresteia*, our only surviving "trilogy," the connection among the three tragedies entered in 458 (*Agamemnon, Choephoroi, Eumenides*) is so deliberate that, if only the *Eumenides* survived, we would not be in a position interpret it as the final play of the trilogy. The satyr play of the "tetralogy" was the *Proteus*, a divine figure from the *Odyssey* connected with Menelaos' return home and, therefore, with Aeschylus' trilogic history of the House of Atreus. In the case of Euripides' *Trojan Women* we have the last play of a tragic "trilogy" preceded by *Alexandros, Palamedes*, and followed by the satyr play, *Sisyphos*. It has been convincingly argued from the considerable evidence for the first two tragedies of the group that this "Trojan trilogy" constitutes Euripides' only coherent attempt to produce three plays with close thematic and dramatic connections.[9] What this means is that the last play of the trilogy relied for its full effect on the audience's immediate knowledge of the two plays that preceded it.

We have more materials for reconstructing the *Alexandros* than for either *Palamedes* or *Sisyphos*. Because of the sententiousness of his speakers, memorable lines from Euripides are often excerpted by anthologists. Language from his choruses usually survives, if it survives at all, in papyrus fragments. There are also papyri giving the arguments of some of the plays of Euripides (known as "Tales from Euripides") and accounts of the legends he worked with (and might have influenced) by mythographers such as Hyginus and Apollodorus. In the case of the *Alexandros* we have a papyrus argument, lyric fragments in papyrus, quotation, and a mythographic

---

8   I make a fuller presentation of what is preserved of the *Alexandros, Palamedes*, and
      the satyr play *Sisyphos* in Appendix 1.
9   By Ruth Scodel, *The Trojan Trilogy of Euripides* (Hypomnemata 60), Göttingen
      1980. She pursued the argument made by Gilbert Murray first in 1932 and then
      in a fuller and more satisfactory form in "Euripides' Tragedies of 415 B. C.: The
      Deceitfulness of Life," in *Greek Studies* (Oxford 1946) 127-48.

summary.[10] The background of the play is set out by the speaker of the Prologue (perhaps Aphrodite): to avert the portent of an ominous dream Hecuba had during her pregnancy, King Priam gives the infant Alexander (as he is called) to a herder to expose on Mount Ida. The herder pities the infant and brings him up as Paris. Hecuba is disconsolate over the loss of her baby, and she and Priam establish annual funeral games in his honor.

When he has grown into a young man, Paris, unrecognized as Alexander, competes in these games and is victorious over Hector and other sons of Priam. Because he is a slave and because of his innate arrogance towards his fellow herders, he is brought before Priam and denounced by Deiphobos, a son of Priam and the husband of Helen after the death of Paris (cf. *Trojan Women* 959-60). It seems that Paris is acquitted. But he is not out of danger. Out of concern for the position of their family, Deiphobos and Hecuba plot to murder Paris. His death is prevented by the confession of the herder who brought him up.

We do not know how the judgment of Paris was treated in the *Alexandros*. Paris' choice of Aphrodite over her rivals, Athena and Hera, is referred to in *The Trojan Women* (by Helen in 923-37 and by Hecuba in 969-90); it was probably described in the Prologue to the *Alexandros*. The chorus of this play consisted of Trojan women close to Hecuba and the palace; there is evidence for a subsidiary chorus (*parachoregema*) of Paris' fellow herdsmen. A papyrus fragment in Strasbourg has a scene in which a speaker attempts to console Hecuba for the loss of her new-born son, and the anthologist, Stobaeus, cites commonplaces of consolation from Euripides' *Alexandros*. Both *Alexandros* and *Trojan Women* have choruses of Trojan women, but only in the first play of the "trilogy" is consolation possible.

Next comes the *Palamedes*. It is set sometime before the action of the *Iliad*. It begins with the quarrel between Achilles and Agamemnon in the tenth year of the war. The point of view of both the *Alexandros* and *Trojan Women* is Trojan; the action takes place at Troy. The point of view of *Palamedes* is Greek; the action takes place in the Greek camp outside the walls of Troy. We know nothing about the lyrics of the chorus, but the chorus must consist of Greek soldiers. Of the characters, we know of Odysseus (who must speak the Prologue to reveal his plot against Palamedes); a soldier of Odysseus who reports Palamedes' treasonable correspondence to Agamemnon; Palamedes; Agamemnon, who acts as judge of the charges Odysseus brings against Palamedes; a messenger who probably reports on the execution of

---

10 See Scodel 1980: 20-42 and my treatment in Appendix 1.

Palamedes; and his brother Oiax, who comes to Troy after Palamedes has been executed.

In *Palamedes*, Odysseus is well worth watching. He will reappear. Although he does not appear in a speaking role in *The Trojan Women*, he is the engineer of the strategem of the Trojan horse and he persuades the Greek army to murder Astyanax. Hecuba is alotted to him as a slave. His role in *Palamedes* and his off-stage machinations in *The Trojan Women* prepare for the appearance of Sisyphos in the satyr play that closes this tetralogy. According to tragic traditions hostile to Odysseus (including Sophocles' *Philoctetes* of 409), Sisyphos and not Laertes was the father of Odysseus.[11] As in the case of Sophocles' *Philoctetes*, where Odysseus frames the plot to bring Philoctetes to Troy, Odysseus is the contriver of the plot of the *Palamedes*. This is to turn Palamedes' invention of writing against him by composing a forged letter to Priam to convict a dangerous rival of treason. To corroborate his frame-up of Palamedes, Odysseus has Trojan gold buried in his tent in his absence. There are, as one would expect, additional complexities in a plot devised by Odysseus (and Euripides), but *Palamedes* seems to add something to the "Trojan trilogy" that prepares the audience for the action of *The Trojan Women*: sophistry. Odysseus is actuated by two motives: resentment and rivalry. He resents Palamedes because it was Palamedes who exposed Odysseus' feigned madness on Ithaka to avoid having to join the expedition against Troy; he is jealous of Palamedes because, as the inventor of the arts of civilization (including writing), he threatens to outshine Odysseus as an intellectual (*sophistes*).[12]

Two illustrations will serve to demonstrate how the plays of the "trilogy" connect. First: in the Prologue of the *Alexandros* (whoever delivers it), Hecuba's dream is described as an essential part of the background of the play. She dreamt that she gave birth to a torch from which snakes flared out, an evil omen for Troy that Priam attempts to abort. He gives the infant to a herdsman to do away with, but Alexander is saved by the herdsman and grows up to be the cause of Troy's destruction (cf. *Trojan Women* 922). The torch Hecuba saw

---

11   See *Philoctetes* 417; this genealogy can be taken back to Aeschylus' *Decision over the Arms*, fr. 175 Radt (texts and translation in the appendix of Hugh Lloyd-Jones to Herbert Weir Smith's *Aeschylus II* [London . Cambridge, Massachusetts 1971] 438-41). In Plato's *The Apology of Socrates*, Socrates is eager to interview both Odysseus and Sisyphos in the Underworld (41C).

12   The importance of intelligence and the title *sophos* (wise, or, in its debased sense, clever) in the Palamedes plays of Aeschylus, Sophocles, Euripides, and the *Prometheus* of Aeschylus is properly stressed by Dana Ferrin Sutton in *Two Lost Plays of Euripides* (New York 1987) 126-29.

in her dream was an omen. It appears as a reality when it is sighted by the Trojan women at the end of the "trilogy," as Greek soldiers put torches to the walls of Troy (1256-8 and 1318). Second: In the first lines of the *Alexandros*, Troy is described as "famous" (*kleinon*). As the god-built walls of this "famous" city collapse in flame and ashes, Troy survives only in tragedy, even as the chorus lament that its "famous name" has perished (*The Trojan Women* 1278).

Torches and fame are thematic connections. There are also connections that are intellectual and dramatic. Each of the three plays of Euripides' "Trojan trilogy" features an *agon* or contest.[13] In *Alexandros*, the *agon* pits Paris, who is taken to be a slave and, thus, in Greek terms, ineligible to compete in athletic contests, against his brother Deiphobos, soon to succeed him as Helen's husband. An angry and defeated Deiphobos denounces Paris before Priam. Paris, who will soon be revealed as free born and a prince, makes the case for the nobility of the slave in terms that so impressed the anthologist John of Stobi (Stobaeus) that some of his speech survives. The *agon* of *Palamedes* is judicial and involves Odysseus as prosecutor and Palamedes as defendant. The appeal of this trial of two clever men before Agamemnon and the Greek army was irresistible to two of Euripides' contemporaries. One of them wrote a *Defense of Palamedes*; the other a speech *Against Palamedes*. Gorgias, the author of the *In Praise of Helen* (translated in Appendix 2), defended Palamedes, and his pupil, Alkidamas, who responded by acting as plaintiff and composing Odysseus' brief against Palamedes.[14] The last of these tragic contests (*agones*) comes in *The Trojan Women* when Helen and Hecuba square off in a debate over who is responsible for the destruction of Troy. Now Menelaos, and not Agamemnon, sits as judge and the conclusion of the debate is foregone, once Menelaos has become reacquainted with the beauty of a wife he has not seen for ten years. Helen breaks with judicial procedure and speaks first, anticipating the charges that will be leveled against her (914-65). After the chorus remark that Helen speaks well but acts badly,[15] Hecuba responds to all of her arguments, except her charge that Hecuba

---

13   This crucial *agones* of the three plays are well assessed by Scodel, 1980: 80-104.

14   A translation of Gorgias' speech can be found in Rosamond Kent Sprague, *The Older Sophists* (Indianapolis . Cambridge, Massachusetts 2001) 54-63; Alkidamas' speech is translated by J. V. Muir in *Alkidamas: The Works & Fragments* (London 2001) 20-33. Aeschylus had staged a very similar *agon* between Odysseus and Ajax over their competing claims for the arms of Achilles and the title "best of the Achaeans" in *The Decision over the Arms*. Only fragments of this play survive.

15   Repeating the words of Palamedes after Odysseus had spoken, fr. 883 in August Nauck, *Tragicorum Graecorum Fragmenta* (second edition 1887). For a translation of the surviving texts of this *agon*, see Appendix 1.

herself was responsible for the destruction of Troy, since she gave birth to the firebrand that has destroyed Troy (919-22). Hecuba's long speech (969-1032) lifts her far above the inarticulate sounds of grief with which she begins to speak. Helen's defense relies conspicuously on Gorgias' praise of her. Menelaos sentences his offending wife to death. But any reader of the *Odyssey* is familiar with the scene of Menelaos and Helen rejoined in Sparta in their autumnal middle age. The debate scene in *The Trojan Women* might seem incongruously sophistic and out of place in a play that dramatizes bereavement. But it might be another indication of Euripides' appreciation of the only power the powerless possess: language and poetry.[16]

4 Dramaturgy

In staging *The Trojan Women* Euripides was granted the same resources as his rivals: three actors, an oboe player (*auletes*), and a chorus of fifteen. He also employed a number of actors who did not speak. Astyanax is one of these. All actors in Athenian tragedy were men. Now we remember Katherine Hepburn as Hecuba and Irene Pappas as Helen in Michael Cacoyannis' *The Trojan Women* (1971). It comes as a shock to realize that the actors who played the part of Hecuba and Helen were the male protagonist and deuteragonist (the first and second actors—or, in Greek, competitors). Hecuba is on stage from the beginning of the play to its end. In the Prologue, the second actor plays the part of Poseidon and the third actor the part of Athena. Then, the assignment of roles is straightforward: in the first episode the deuteragonist plays the challenging part of Kassandra; the tritagonist (or third actor) the part of Talthybios. In the next two episodes, the second actor plays the part of Andromache and Helen, and the tritagonist the parts of Talthybios and Menelaos. The human actors move on stage. The gods stand on a platform above the stage, the *theologeion*. This platform represents the walls of Troy. The chorus files into the orchestra in two groups (*hemichoroi*) during the entrance song (Parodos). They have joined and taken their place in the orchestra during the three *stasima* (or choral passages) that follow. Actors and chorus all wear masks.

Formally, The Trojan Women has the articulations of every Greek tragedy. It is constructed out of familiar building blocks: a Prologue spoken by a god which gives, as is Euripides' manner, the background of the action of the play and an intimation of its outcome.

---

16   "Speech," Gorgias claims in his *In Praise of Helen* §8, "is a mighty Master" (the full text can be found in Appendix 2). Speech is a master even for those who in Euripides' *Trojan Women* are enslaved.

This is followed by the *Parodos*, or the entrance song of the chorus as they occupy their place in the orchestra of the Theater of Dionysos after they have entered through the *parodos* (or lateral entranceway). The Prologue is spoken in iambic trimeters, the formalized rhythm of speech used throughout the play. The Parodos involves a lyric exchange between the chorus of fifteen (young men dressed as) women and Hecuba. They speak in the first person singular, and sing in the Doric dialect in a variety of meters employed only for the song and dance of lyric poetry accompanied by the *aulos* (in range, the oboe). From their entrance song, speech alternates with song and *epeisodia* with *stasima* until the final scene of the play, or *Exodos* (exit). If tragedy originated out of the dithyramb,[17] a circular dance which, in Athens, was performed by a leader and a chorus of forty-nine young men or adults, the original meaning of the term *epeisodion* becomes clearer: these are the "interludes" of speech between two or among three actors "interrupting" song and dance. Literally, a *stasimon* is a song performed by the chorus when they have taken their position or "stand" in the orchestra.

The Trojan Women is structurally unusual (if any of our nineteen surviving tragedies can be said to be unusual) in its use of the half choruses of the *Parodos* and the lyric and antiphonal exchanges between Hecuba and Andromache in the second episode. And, as the chorus look for a god to appear on the walls of Troy to release them from their fate as slaves to their Greek conquerors, no god appears on the platform known as the *theologeion*.

Prologue and Exodos   The scene that opens *The Trojan Women* has the Prologue familiar from the tragedies of Euripides. The stage of the action of the play is set by Poseidon, a god who, with the help of Apollo, built the walls of Troy for King Laomedon. He addresses the audience directly and pays no attention to the woman in black writhing on stage below. It is only at line 36 that he looks down to "this poor creature." Poseidon is leaving "famous" (*kleinon*) Troy. His reasons are simple and expedient (28-9):

> When a terrible desolation takes a city,
> the world of the gods sickens and will not receive its
>   honors.

These words are the beginning of the theology of *The Trojan Women*, a theology most fully expressed by the chorus who have come to realize that all their tendance of the gods has not protected

---

their city from utter destruction. At the end of the play they look up to the walls on which Poseidon stood as the play opened, as if hoping for salvation from some Euripidean *deus ex machina*. Prologue and Exodos mark the beginning and end of Euripides' treatment of the gods who protect cities, but who are fundamentally indifferent to their human votaries.

Hecuba   Hecuba is on stage, either prostrate or standing, throughout the play. Her language can be plotted on a scale: silence; inarticulate sounds of grief (*aiai aiai, omoi, oimoi, io, pheu, pheu*); the agonized, antiphonal lyrics of the Parodos accompanied by her rocking body; her sober dealings with an ecstatic daughter (Kassandra); her cold advice to the wife of her son Hector (Andromache); and her calculating response to Helen's speech in her own defense. The final scene of the play ("Astyanax") is the moment of her greatest dramatic power, as she bends down over the small broken body of her grandson and recalls his childhood, his father, and laments the life he will not have.

Formally, her first lyric monologue is part of the Prologue. It bears some resemblance to the monologue of Hecuba in the Prologue to the Hecuba (59-97) in its meter (it is heavily anapestic), situation, and context. In the Hecuba (of the 420s), Hecuba has just been visited by the ghost of her murdered son, Polydoros, and is surrounded by a group of captive Trojan women. In *The Trojan Women* the barely articulate grief of Hecuba contrasts with the calm, calculating, and literally elevated language of the two gods who stand on the walls of Troy. The anapestic rhythm of her speech is a vigorous marching measure that contrasts violently with her status as a prisoner and the pain that racks her body.

Hecuba bears the burden of grief and loss in the play. As the play opens, she has lost Priam, who was slaughtered at the altar of Zeus in their palace enclosure (481-83); and she has lost her sons (480-82). When she asks the herald from the Greek army about the fate of her youngest daughter, she does not understand that Polyxena had been slaughtered too, at Achilles' tomb (260-68; cf. 622-29) (See Fig. 2). She goes on to face her own fate as the drudge of Odysseus on Ithaka (277); the loss of Kassandra, who had already been dragged from the altar of Athena by Ajax, son of Oileus (70, 171); of Hector's wife, Andromache, who will be taken away by Achilles' son; and her grandson, Astyanax, whose body is brought to her for burial on the shield of his father.

Another theme announced in Hecuba's monody is that of the power of poetry, a poetry that rises from the inarticulate but meaningful sounds of lamentation to the lyrics that are the monuments commemorating human loss. This is the "Muse of

*Figure 2: The Polyxena Sarcophagus, from the Troad ca. 520-500 B. C.
Copyright Project Troia, University of Tübingen*

misery" (120). This poetry, which begins as threnody, is the only thing over which the victims of war have any control. Even the argument Hecuba urges against Helen is an expression of the power of the powerless. The chorus recognize the pleasure and power of lament in two passages: first as they join in the antiphonal lament and respond to Hecuba's lament (608-9):

> Yes, tears are sweet to those in trouble
> and the heart-rending strain of lamentation and the
>   Muse of suffering.

This is the pleasure and consolation of the present. There is also the consoling thought that in the future they will be the theme of song (1242-45):[18]

> Yet, had not some god turned our world upside down
> and buried our towers in the earth, we would have been
>   ciphers.
> We would never have been the subject of song;
> we would never have provided an argument
> for the Muse of mortal poets yet to be born.

---

18   These passages are well treated by Charles Segal in a larger context, *Euripides and the Poetics of Sorrow: Art, Gender, and Commemoration in Alcestis, Hippolytus, and Hecuba*, Durham . London 1993.

Kassandra Kassandra is the first of three women who will enter the stage as deuteragonist to Hecuba. She acts on center stage in the first episode of *The Trojan Women*, a play that is open to Aristotle's criticism of the "episodic" plot, in which one action follows another without a plausible or necessary connection.[19] But the episodic character of *The Trojan Women* should not be counted a fault. Andromache follows Kassandra on stage in the second episode and Helen, Kassandra in the third; finally the small body of Astyanax is brought in stage in the final "episode" of the Exodos. All these episodes have an intimate and necessary connection, as the fate and character of the women who have been reserved for the commanders of the army are brought out from their tents to take leave of Hecuba and prepare for their forced departure from Troy. These scenes are "tragic" in Aristotle's conception of tragedy, for they reveal and provoke the tragic emotions of pity and fear. Aristotle was accurate to his own conception of tragedy when he called Euripides "the most tragic" of tragedians.[20]

Kassandra had played a prophetic role in the *Alexandros*. She plays a prophetic role here as well. Her situation is ambiguous. The torch she waves over her head in ecstasy is not the instrument of her self-immolation and it is not a marriage torch, except as the symbol that her "marriage" will be to Hades, the bridegroom of young women who die unmarried.[21] Her mother is no more capable of understanding her gestures and language than are the other Trojans. Kassandra is driven and divided by two divine forces: Apollo, the god of prophecy, and Dionysos, the god of ecstasy.[22] More immediately, she had been dragged from the altar and cult statue of Athena by Ajax, son of Oileus (69-71).[23] This scene is depicted in the interior of a large cup now in the Villa Giulia Museum, Rome, showing in its interior the rape of Kassandra and the murder of Priam, at the altar of Zeus of the Enclosure. What is particularly grim about this last scene on the inner tondo (or rim) is the instrument by which Neoptolemos

---

19   *Poetics* 9.1451b33-33.

20   *Poetics* 13.1453a30, where he concedes that Euripides is not a master of plot construction; see Segal, 1993: 25-29.

21   For the prevalent connection of marriage and death in Greek culture, see Rush Rehm, *Marriage to Death: The Conflation of Wedding and Funeral Rituals in Greek Tragedy*, Princeton 1994, especially Chapter 9.

22   See the notes to lines 329 and 408. Clearly she is presented as a Maenad, or ecstatic female votary of Dionysos. The only scene in Homer where Maenads are mentioned is that describing the overpowering grief of Hecuba at the death of Hector, as she is compared to a Maenad, *Iliad* 22.460.

23   This scene from the post-Homeric Sack of Troy (*Iliupersis*) has its lyric treatment in a poem preserved in two papyrus fragments of Alcaeus, David A. Campbell, *Greek Lyric Poetry I: Sappho and Alcaeus* (Loeb Classical Library), (Cambridge, Massachusetts and London 1984), no. 298 (pp. 338-41).

Figure 3: Ajax the Lesser raping Cassandra. *Tondo of an Attic red-figure cup, ca. 440–430 B. C., by Kodros-Maler. Louvre Compana Collection, 1861. Photo © Bibi Saint-Pol / Wikimedia Commons.*

kills Priam: the dead body of Astyanax. The outer surface of the cup shows two scenes of the warfare outside the walls of Troy: Briseis being led away from Achilles and the duel of Hector and Ajax.

Kassandra is capable of stepping out of her bacchant's dance (366) and placing before her grieving mother the paradox that the Trojans are more fortunate than the Achaeans (364-77). Her "demonstration" borders on (and was meant to suggest) sophistry. It is not on the level of Andromache's proof that Polyxena is happier dead than alive (635-42) or Helen's outrageous speech of exculpation in which she provokes the jury in Euripides' theater by claiming that Hecuba and Priam were actually responsible for the Trojan War (914-22). Kassandra's reckoning involves first the cost of the war to the Greeks (365-405) and then the countervailing advantages of the Trojans. In her powerful statement of the cost of war to the Greeks, Kassandra is not wrong. The serious lesson invested in her "demonstration" is that in war there are no victors: only suffering. Kassandra then turns to the hidden present to predict the future sufferings of Odysseus on his way home from Troy and at home in Ithaka (431-42); she finally reverts to her earlier mode of prophetic frenzy, as she foresees her own death in Argos (445-61).

Andromache The second episode might be entitled "Andromache." Andromache now takes center stage. She and her son are carried onto the stage on a cart laden with other spoils of war. Andromache and Astyanax have been reduced to chattel. This scene resembles the "Kassandra" episode in one respect. Just as Kassandra moves from bacchic frenzy to a balanced calculation of the fortune of Troy set against the fortune of the Greeks, Andromache moves from the long antiphonal and lyric lament with Hecuba (577-633) to the paradoxical argument that Polyxena is more fortunate than she (634-83). Her careful articulation of "those qualities that are found admirable in a woman" to prove that she was the perfect wife (645-79) concludes her long and seemingly incongruous speech to her mother-in-law.

A little more than a decade before Euripides staged *The Trojan Women*, Andromache's "ideal" had been voiced by Pericles in his speech at the state funeral for those who had fallen during the first year of the Peloponnesian War. He has virtually nothing to say to the women in his audience. His parting words—which come almost as an afterthought—are not to mothers who had lost sons to war or the daughters who had been orphaned by it, but to the new widows of Athens: "If I am obliged to say something about the virtue of a woman [or: of even a woman] to those who are now widows, let me compress my remarks into a single piece of advice. Your greatest claim to a good reputation is not to be inferior to your nature. Your greatest glory is to be spoken of least among men—either for your virtue or your vices" (*The Peloponnesian War*, 2.45). It is precisely and ironically the talk of Andromache's "virtue" in the Greek army that destroyed her (657). In Euripides' *Andromache* this ideal had been voiced by Andromache herself, who would not only prevent women from leaving the house and being seen in public; she would not even allow other women within her house, "for they are the tutors of mischief" (943).

More than misogyny, justly or unjustly imputed, is involved in these lines. In this play Euripides is concerned with exploring just what power the weak and helpless possess. Unlike Kassandra, Andromache does not face death; nor can she look forward to Helen's autumnal and golden years of amnesty and amnesia. Her fate is that of a widow and slave. She will be forced to live under the same roof as the son of the man whose father killed both her husband (Hector) and her father (Eetion). And she will live the "hostage syndrome" of forming an attachment to and dependence on her new master. Her third and last marriage to her countryman, Helenos, only glimmers on the far horizon of her life and is not glimpsed in *The Trojan Women*.[24]

---

24   This marriage is glanced at in Euripides, *Andromache* 1264 and Aeneas meets
      her with Helenos at Buthrotum on the coast of north-west Greece, Virgil, *Aeneid*
      2.294-6.

Helen   The third episode (860-1059) centers on Helen. In staging and in costume Euripides offers a characterization of Helen and Menelaos which is as effective and dramatic as anything said on stage. *Opsis*, or spectacle, is one of the crucial elements of this episode. We first see Menelaos and his men from the Achaean army enter the stage. Menelaos delivers a brave address to the sun and the audience, but he speaks to no one in particular until he gives orders to his men to go into the tent and drag Helen out by the hair (880-2). When Helen emerges from the tent, she is elegantly dressed and her hair is carefully arranged. The contrast with Hecuba and the other mourning women in black is stark and offensive. Hecuba gives the director of *The Trojan Women* directions when she expresses her outrage at Helen's conduct after the death of her "husband" Paris (1023-7):

> And afterwards, you appeared in public like this,
> beautifully dressed and carefully made up; and you look
>   upon the same sky
> as your husband. I could spit upon you!
> You ought to have come out humble, your eyes to the
>   ground,
> in the torn garments of a widow, with your hair shorn in
>   the Scythian fashion.

Even as she crosses the Aegean, presumably on her way to her death in Sparta, the chorus imagine Helen as seated contemplating her image in a golden mirror (1107-8).

It is true that Helen indignantly protests her rough treatment: "Menelaos, this rude treatment announces some dreadful thing!" (895). But a director would know better than to treat her with violence. Vase painters were well aware of the dramatic potential of the scene when, after ten years of absence, Menelaos confronts his wayward wife. They show him dropping his sword at the sight of her. Perhaps the most striking representation of this scene is on a gladiator's parade helmet from Pompeii. In Euripides' play, Menelaos and his men stand at a respectful and admiring distance from her.

There are no sounds of mourning in the Helen episode, but, as in the Kassandra and Andromache episodes, there is a set speech urging a paradox: that Helen is innocent of leaving Menelaos for Paris and that Priam and Hecuba are the guilty causes of Troy's destruction. The great judicial *agon* with Menelaos as judge has been introduced in our treatment of Euripides' "Trojan trilogy." Helen speaks first; then Hecuba attempts to refute her. Helen breaks with judicial conventions in that she speaks first, before the accusation against her has been heard. Neither Menelaos or Hecuba object. In anticipating the speech of the prosecution, Helen formulates the charges against her in her own terms. Not only does she shift blame for her flight from Sparta and the Trojan War on others—Hecuba, Priam, Aphrodite, and even Menelaos himself ("you craven coward!" 943); she praises herself for having saved Greece from barbarian hegemony (932-37). She makes Menelaos agree to her claim that a god compelled her to follow Paris when she deals with the charge that she should have left Troy after the death of Paris: "At that time my marriage was not compassed by a god" (943). She even calls upon the watchmen at the gates and sentinels on the ramparts as witnesses that she then attempted to escape (955). These witnesses, of course, cannot testify on her behalf; they are all dead.

Astyanax   In Greek tragedy, there were characters on stage who did not speak. In Aristophanes' *Frogs* (911-13) the comic character Euripides complains of Aeschylus' use of silent characters (known as *koupha prosopa*). But no silent character in Greek tragedy has a more powerful role than does Astyanax, whose broken body is brought on stage by Greek soldiers, who themselves do not speak. His death prompts the thought of what his life would have been and the memory of what his father's life had been. Talthybios' report of the fear of the Greek army that son would grow up to be like his father (724) resembles the fear of the tyrant Eyrystheus that Herakles' sons would grow up to be like their father (Euripides, *The Sons of Herakles* 468-70). In this final scene, we are left not only with grief: we are meant to recall the contests over nobility already staged in the *Alexandros* and *Palamedes*. Finally, we are left in the world of Odysseus.

The Chorus: The Power of Lamentation (**Kommos***):*   The formality of the antiphonal song exchanged between Hecuba and the chorus in this movement of the Parodos is alien to European poetic traditions, but it was very much a part of the long Greek tradition of ritual lament, a family duty and prerogative that belonged entirely to women in the world of ancient (and modern) Greece.[25]

The Parodos of *The Trojan Women* is already familiar. *Parodos* in Greek has two meanings: the entrance into the orchestra of the theater and the entrance song of the chorus. The chorus enter in two groups

---

25   An illustration of this tradition comes from an Attic black-figure vase
     [*loutrophoros*] of the Sappho painter and ca. 500 B. C. This shows the corpse of
     a warrior laid out in state; his widow or mother holding his head; and a line
     of women in black and lamentation. This vase should be studied with other
     figures in Margaret Alexiou's *The Ritual Lament in the Greek Tradition*, Cambridge:
     Cambridge University Press 1974 (Figure 1). A similar scene, from another black-
     figure vase now in the Louvre is the appropriate illustration on the cover of
     Shirley A. Barlow's *Euripides: The Trojan Women*: Warminster, Wiltshire 1986.

Figure 4: Fresco from The Villa Villoresi, Colonnata. Odysseus, Andromache, and Astyanax. Photo: Courtesy of Contessa Cristina Villoresi

and respond to Hecuba's laments (all in lyric meter). Hecuba's position on the ground is that of a mourning woman. What can be added to the formal analysis of the Parodos is the shift in the strophe (197-213) from the Greece of Corinth, Athens, and Sparta as destinations to the Vale of Tempe, Olympos, Sicily, and south Italy in the antistrophe (214-29). In the *Hecuba* the chorus move from thoughts of Lacedaemon and Phthia in the strophe—both hostile nations (444-53), to thoughts of Delos in the antistrophe—the sacred site of the cult of Apollo (454-65). In the final strophe they end with the choice of Athens where they could serve as *ergastinai*, the cult title of the Athenian women of important families who contributed to the quadrennial festival of Athena by weaving a *peplos*, as the Trojan captives had done in Troy (466-74).[26] The concentration on Athens in both plays creates a Greek world that is both anachronistic and Athenocentric.

Stasimon 1: The Fall of Troy This the first full choral song of *The Trojan Women*; the chorus has joined as a whole to perform it. In their entry song (*parodos*), they had been divided into two groups and their singing was antiphonal to Hecuba's lamentation. This lamentation (*kommos*) carries over into this song, which they begin by

---

26 The Trojan women's gift of a *peplos* placed on the cult statue of Athena on the acropolis of Troy is described in *Iliad* 6.271-3 and 287-311.

Figure 5: Mykonos Vase (Archeological Museum of Mykonos),
depicting one of the earliest known renditions of the Trojan
Horse. Photo by Traveling Runes. CC BY- SA 2.0.

an invocation to a Muse, asking her to sing "in a new strain" (514). The
invocation is epic (in dactylic meter) and it commemorates a moment
in the Trojan War that lies beyond the range of the *Iliad* (but not the
Odyssey)—the moment that seemed to mark the triumph of the Trojans
in their defensive war of ten years. This anthem is new too in its point
of view. It does not look back upon the event it commemorates from
the vantage of a remote and impersonal memory; it is the expression
of a group of captive women's experience of the disaster in which they
are still involved. The world within Troy is reflected in the personal
inner world of the chorus and its memory.

    Another tragic text that contains an ominous prediction of the
fate of the Greek victors who did not respect the shrines and temples
of "sacred Ilion" (see the note to line 123) is Aeschylus' *Agamemnon*
where Clytemnestra says of the victorious army (338-42):

> If they treat with reverence the gods who hold the city,
> the gods of this captured city, and what is sacred to the
>   gods,
> what they have destroyed will not come to life again.
> Let no lust possess the armies,

> Let them not destroy what they must not destroy
> and become captives to their greed.

The messenger from the Greek army in Troy makes the fate of the victorious clear as he reports (527-8):

> The altars of the gods have vanished, and the statues
>   and shrines of the gods,
> and the seed of the whole land has been destroyed.

Poseidon ominously repeats Clytemnestra's explicit warning in *The Trojan Women* (95-7). The warning is as relevant in 458, when Aeschylus staged his *Oresteia* as in 415, when Euripides' staged his *Trojan Women*; as it is on May 17, 2004 when I write these words.

In the *Odyssey*, the Trojan horse is seen from the point of view of the trials of the warriors within and of Odysseus especially (in the war memories of Menelaos, 4. 272-89 and Odysseus, 9. 523-32). In this choral ode, the Trojan horse is seen from without and the sack of Troy, from within. The Trojan horse, the product of the skill of Epeios and the strategy of Odyssey, "the child of Athena's cunning" (560), is an emblem of the deceptiveness of proud appearances. To the Trojans it seems a magnificent gift, with its cheek-piece of gold; but it is pregnant with death within. In an instant the reality within the horse is revealed, and the victory festival of torches, song, and dancing into the night is transformed into the horror of a city sacked. The powerful and latent ambiguities of this scene—with its black and white contrast between appearance and reality—are well expressed by the "dark radiance" of the hearth fires within the houses of the sleeping Trojans.

Stasimon 2: Salamis, Athens, Ganymede, Tithonos (799-859)[27]
This choral ode divides into two sets of strophe and antistrophe. The first strophe and antistrophe look back to the first Greek expedition against the Troy of Laomedon and, only at the end of the first antistrophe, is the destruction of the Troy of his son, Priam, alluded to (817-19). In the second strophe and antistrophe, the chorus suddenly shift from a city twice destroyed to heaven and the love of Zeus for Trojan Ganymede and the love of the goddess of the dawn (Eos) for the Trojan Tithonos. But there is a residue of Trojan grief and loss in both strophe and antistrophe, and it becomes the more bitter as the joy and serenity of life in heaven is contrasted with life on earth. The

---

27 There is a revealing study of this ode by Anne Pippin Burnett, "*Trojan Women* and the Ganymede Ode," *Yale Classical Studies* 25 (1977) 291-316.

order of Ganymede followed by Tithonos is already established in the Homeric *Hymn to Aphrodite* (202-10; 210-27).

The chorus begin by evoking Salamis and, strangely enough, Athens on the mainland opposite. In the generation before the Trojan War, Telamon (brother of Peleus and father of Ajax, and king of the island of Salamis) joined Herakles in the first Greek assault on Troy. For his efforts he received Hesione, daughter of Laomedon, as a slave. In the first stasimon (511-30), the chorus sang of the fall of Troy in a single night. Now they move back a generation. They are not, however, acting as historians to Euripides' audience. The first strophe of the Ganymede ode has a single function: that is to display the all too human physiognomy of the Greek gods that ranges from ardent rapture to cold indifference. Eros, the god of sexual passion, has joined heaven and earth in the passion of Zeus for Ganymede and of Eos (the goddess of the dawn) for Tithonos. The putative "bond" is termed a *kedos* (845). This is the Greek word for the bond created by marriage; it establishes a mutual concern between two groups that are not related by blood. The word also means a funeral.

We have already examined the Pindaric and epinician language that attaches Athens to Salamis and Athens to Troy. But we have not commented on the Pindaric background of the language the chorus choose to describe Athens. One possible reading of these passages in which Greek lands are described in the epinician language of praise is that Euripides is writing what Pindar wrote in only one of his epinician odes (*Pythian* VII for Megalkes of Athens)—a praise of Athens, whose ennobling epithets, "renowned", "blessed", "sacred land of Theseus, where divinity dwells", seems to recall the language that once described the "sacred," "famous" (*kleinon*), and prosperous city of Troy. At some point of his career as a tragic poet, Euripides wrote an epinician ode to celebrate the victories of Alcibiades.[28] It is plausible that his praise of Alcibiades involved a praise of Athens. But let us face still another possibility; that Euripides' epinician praise of Athens is designed to place his native city on the high pedestal of the victor. Standing on this pedestal is both a privileged and a precarious position.

Athens of the first strophe belongs to the remote world of Ganymede and Tithonos and stands in sharp contrast to Troy. Athens is favored by the very divinity that was first hostile, then friendly, to Troy, Athena. On the acropolis of Athens Athena "revealed" the branch of olive to mankind (804). In this ode this olive branch is not a symbol of peace but it is plaited into the crown of the victor. The acropolis is sacred (802) and Athens prosperous (804), as once was Troy.

---

28   An ode known to Plutarch (*Alcibiades* 11).

Ganymede is recalled in the antistrophe. The Euripidean contrast between the undisturbed and serene joy of heaven, where Ganymede is employed as the cup-bearer of Zeus, and the pain of the mortals left in desolation upon the plain of the Troad is already present in the Homeric *Hymn to Aphrodite*. Here the bliss of Ganymede's life in heaven is contrasted with his father's grief over the loss of his son (202-10). Euripides seems intent on contradicting the theology of the Homeric hymn. In this ode there is no hint of Zeus's pity for Ganymede's father or the happy ending in what Aphrodite tells her mortal husband, the Trojan Anchises, of Zeus's recompense for the loss of a son by the gift of a team of horses (210-27).[29] The bliss of Zeus and Ganymede as they lift up towards heaven is beautifully rendered in an Archaic terra cotta group now in the Olympia Museum.

Figure 6: Late Archaic terracotta statue of Zeus and Ganymede, Olympia Archaeological Museum. Photo by Joan Banjo. CC BY-SA 3.0.

But the gods are not concerned with those to whom they are related as *kedestai* (or the ties not of blood but of "marriage"). The pious service of Ganymede as steward in the halls of the feasting gods (824-5) is worthless to Troy. On Olympos he walks softly in his luxuriant pride while his city burns. And Eos, the heavenly goddess who had conceived a passion for the Trojan Tithonos, carried him off to heaven, and had a son by him (Memnon), looks down from her radiance upon the fires consuming Troy with divine indifference.

Stasimon 3: Sacred Ilion This final stasimon of the play continues and develops the theology first announced in Poseidon's

---

29   The theme of immortal horses seems a part of the "trilogy." There is, of course, the Trojan Horse. Athena is called goddess of immortal horses in the first stasimon (536 and note) and the mares of the savage king of Thrace, Diomedes, figured in the *Sisyphos*.

speech in the Prologue and brilliantly revealed in the "Ganymede Ode" of the second *stasimon*. In this final choral song, the captive women of Troy divide the world into three levels: the shimmering and remote heights occupied by the gods; the underworld; and, in between, the earth which is the site of living humans as they attempt to reach both the indifferent gods on high and their dead below. In the first strophe and antistrophe the chorus call upon Zeus and remind the gods of the pious attempts of their city to join heaven and earth and assure the prosperity and safety of Troy. In the *Iliad*, Troy and its citadel is called "sacred"; its citadel (Pergamos) was the site of the temples of Apollo and Athena.[30]

The Trojan captives begin their song by calling to mind the festivals of their city that once had made it sacred in its contact with Zeus and the gods. The details of their lyrics are all meaningful and informed by a contrast: first of past and present and then, and by implication, of the human and the divine.[31] The altars of Troy are smoking, and the smoke of frankincense "lifts up into the clear blue sky" (1065). The high ridges of Ida are filled with the radiance of the first sacred light of day and this height overlooking Troy on the plain below is seen as "a generous land filled with light and sacred to the gods" (1070). The offerings recalled in the antistrophe—sacrifices, the song and choral dancing of the night festivals of young women, the golden statues of the gods, and the moon-shaped cakes offered to the gods—are human gestures designed to conciliate the divine to the human. The chorus do not mention prayer to the gods. Their address to Zeus is not a prayer but an indignant question. This question is answered by silence and then, at the play's end, by the final collapse of "holy Troy" in flames. The last choral song and dance constitutes a gesture of alienation.

5 Theology

The theology of *The Trojan Women* is introduced on the *theologeion*, or the platform on the walls of Troy from which Poseidon speaks the Prologue and encounters Athena. In the Prologue, Hecuba has nothing to say about the gods as she lies prostrate and in agony beneath the two gods above her. She speaks only of a *daimon*, a powerful, unrecognized divine power that compels her (102). But she

---

30   Ilion (in the form Ilios) is called sacred (*hiere*) twice in the only book of the *Iliad* that allows us to enter the doomed walls of Troy (6.277 and 403). There is a fine study of the meaning of this epithet for Troy in the *Iliad* by Stephen Scully in *Homer and the Sacred City* (Ithaca, New York 1990), Chapter 2.

31   The closest parallel to the contrast of ruin and prosperity is in Aeschylus' *Persians* 249-52. For the larger parallels, see Alexiou 1974: 83-85.

is capable of a more philosophical view of what constitutes divinity as she looks up at the sun Menelaos greets in triumph as Helen has fallen to him, with Troy (884-88):

> You, who bear the weight of the earth and have your
> seat upon the earth,
> whoever you are, hard to know and hard to place.
> Zeus, whether you are the Necessity of Nature or
> Human Intelligence,
> you do I call upon. As you travel your silent course,
> you lead all things human on the path of Justice.

Menelaos' reaction to Hecuba's prayer, a startling innovation to match his own address to the sun (Helios), is one of amazement. Hecuba's precedent for her strange invocation to Zeus as the hidden source of justice in human affairs might be taken back to the invocation to Zeus by the chorus of Aeschylus' *Agamemnon* (160-83). But the alternatives offered by Hecuba as proper descriptions of the true nature of Zeus belong to the last half of the fifth century. Zeus is first seen in Presocratic terms as the fiery element of *aither* (or fiery globe) that surrounds the earth, then as human intelligence or the necessity of nature, terms that have been traced to Anaximenes, Anaxagoras, and Democritus.

The challenge of interpreting these lines is not only that of placing them in their intellectual context in the fifth century; they must also be returned to their context in *The Trojan Women*.[32] What calls for explanation is their apparent incongruity. Immediately, they seem to serve as a foil to Menelaos' complacent dullness. But they also serve to introduce the innovative rhetoric of the age of the sophists —a rhetoric that will become manifest when Helen seeks refuge in Gorgias' *Praise of Helen* to urge her own apology against the charges that will be made against her.

Then there is that moment at the end of the play when Hecuba's conception of Zeus as *aither* and the force that leads all things mortal to justice is belied by the final collapse of Troy, whose smoke ascends like the futile smoke of sacrifice (*knise*) up to a bright and godless *aither* (1298-99 and 1320), a passage now familiar from our analysis of the third *stasimon*. The theology of *The Trojan Women* is articulated by those who know of the justice of Zeus as captives, and who, before the destruction of their city, had worshipped the gods of "holy Troy."

---

32   Two admirable attempts to place them in their context in fifth century thought are those of Scodel, 1980: 93-95 and Charles H. Kahn, "Greek Religion and Philosophy in the Sisyphus Fragment," *Phronesis* 47 (1997) 247-62.

When a terrible desolation takes a city,
The world of the gods sickens and will not receive its
  honors.

The theology of this play is even grimmer than that announced in
Poseidon's farewell to Troy (27-28). For the Trojan women there is no
possibility of a theodicy, or a Miltonic justification of the ways of the
gods towards man. The gods of this play do not finally desert a city
because in its desolation it can no longer offer sacrifice. Despite the
protests of Athena (69), the gods of *The Trojan Women* are remote from
humans and indifferent to human religion. Zeus seems to possess
the only stability present in the world of captured Troy. He sits secure
on his high throne in heaven and its shimmering bright air (1079-80);
but he seems indifferent to, oblivious to "the fierce rush of fire" that
consumes Troy and its temples. In Euripides' Greek the noun *aither* is
echoed in the participle describing the rush of fire that destroys Troy
(*aithomena...horma*, 1080). This last line of the antistrophe answers "the
generous land filled with light and sacred to the gods" (1070).

Does this language imply that the contact between *aither* and
the world of divinity and the human and terrestrial is destructive?
The language of the final scene of the play (the Exodos) seems to
vindicate what is suggested in these words. As for the human world,
the husbands who died in war and the sack of Troy must wander in
death, unburied, unwashed (1082); their widows and children must
make their way as slaves to their various destinations in Greece. The
final wish of the chorus in the last antistrophe of this ode is for the
destruction of Menelaos' ship on its way home. Their wish is never
fulfilled. As for Menelaos, he escapes the fate threatened in the
Prologue for the returning army of Greeks (cf. 77-86); his destiny will
take him to the Islands of the Blest (*Odyssey* 4.561-70). As for Helen,
she faces serene years of dignity and comfort in Sparta (beautifully
described in *Odyssey* 4.120-280).

At the conclusion of Euripides' *Electra*, when Orestes and Electra
stand over the body of the mother they have murdered and are
exposed to the terrible public resentment their matricide will provoke
—in Argos and in the Athenian audience—the chorus suddenly look
up to the roof of the poor house in which the murder has been
committed (1233-37):

But look, there! On the roof of this house
I see two figures. Are they lower spirits
or gods from heaven? This is not the path
of mortal men. What has brought them
to this epiphany before mortal eyes?

As Clytemnestra's twin brothers appear, and Kastor addresses Orestes, Euripides has produced still another sensational ending to a play that has no human solution at its end. One thinks of other plays rescued by a god who appears *ex machina* on top of the stage building to tidy up the insoluble mess of human affairs: the *Medea, Andromache, Heracles, Ion, Helen, Orestes, Antiope,* and still others, including possibly the *Alexandros.*

The "path" of the gods in *The Trojan Women* is the walkway on top of the walls of Troy, where Poseidon meets Athena and looks down upon Hecuba on the stage platform below him. This privileged eminence is the *theologeion,* the place from which the gods speak to the human in the audience. It is elevated above the stage and remote from the scene of human suffering below it. In Euripides' *Hippolytus,* the goddess Artemis appears on the roof of the palace of Troezen. The dying Hippolytus can just catch the scent of her divine presence, yet, as a good goddess, she will not approach death (1392).

In the *Andromache,* the epiphany of Thetis is announced by the chorus of enslaved Trojan women in the same language that the chorus of the *Electra* used to greet the coming of the Dioskouroi (1226-30):

> What is happening now? What divinity do I sense?
> Girls, look, strain your eyes:
> Here is a divinity who is making his passage
> through the white brightness of the sky
> to set foot on the plains of Phthia where horses graze.

In *The Trojan Women* there is no such epiphany of a god or *deus ex machina* appearing on the walls of Troy, where Poseidon and Athena stood as the play opened. Silent Greek soldiers appear on top of these walls and they defeat any hope that a god will appear to save Troy from their flames. A blast from a trumpet signals the departure of the Trojan women. The chorus look up from the stage that has absorbed their attention throughout the play and, as they catch sight of the Greek soldiers above them, they too ask a question:

> What do I see? What men are these
> with torches darting here and there
> on Ilion's fiery crest?
> Some grim new catastrophe
> appends Troy's story.[33]

---

33 This catastrophe is glimpsed in Homer in a striking simile that compares the grief in Troy at the news of Hector's death to the collapse of its walls in flames, *Iliad* 22.410-11, as Adrian Poole once observed, ""Total Disaster: Euripides' *The Trojan Women*," *Arion* New Series 3:3 (1976) 278.

On the Translation   I began this translation in 1975 by producing a "literal" version that was to guide my friend and collaborator, Stephen Berg, in his translation of the play for William Arrowsmith's Greek Tragedy in New Translation series (Oxford University Press). That led to the first collapse of *The Trojan Women*. Our version left Arrowsmith discontented. Two other poets were enlisted to save Troy from the same fate for the same series: Daniel Mark Epstein and Mark Rudman. Both of these versions succumbed to the stern judgment of two editors: Arrowsmith and Herb Golder. In the summer of 2002 I decided to translate the play myself, and take on the roles of both Hellenist and poet. I finish in the summer of 2004.

One of my first challenges was to find a way of conveying the sounds of grief and lamentation. In Greece, the formal and very public drama of lamentation allows the survivors to find an outlet for their grief and, as women (never men) sing and wail in what are now called *moirologia* (songs of fate), they take some control over their fate. The sounds they make—*e e, oi' go, oimoi, omoi, oimoi talaina*, and the strange sigh *pheu*, are untranslatable in English because there is nothing similar in our culture to batten onto. Grief in Anglo-Saxon culture is best expressed by silence, or silent prayer, and in small groups. Or appeals to God! I have attempted to avoid the bathos of "miserable me," "oh, oh," "alack, alas," by leaving a director and audience with the Greek sounds of mourning in italics.

I base my translation on the edition of the Greek text by James Diggle, *Euripidis Fabulae*, volume 2, Oxford 1981. My line numbers closely approximate his, so that a reader who wants to consult the Greek can easily turn to the original. Only rarely do I depart from his text. When I do, or when I have difficulty accepting his text, I usually note my departure and perplexity. Square brackets indicate those passages Diggle and other editors regard as interpolations to the original text. Helpful guides in translating and commenting (if only briefly) on the play are: Léon Parmentier, *Euripide*, vol. 4, Paris 1959 (in the Budé series); Kevin H. Lee, *Euripides: Troades*, London 1976; and Shirley A. Barlow, *Euripides: Trojan Women*, Warminster 1986.

This translation is the product of many years of thinking and meditating on the play in times of war. It is dedicated to my daughters, who I pray will have a better future than the women of Troy. It owes a great debt to the friendship and inspiration of William Arrowsmith, who taught me how, as he described it, to "liquefy the foundations," and make Greek tragedy convincing as dramatic, and, I hope, poetic English, and to visualize the action of *The Trojan Women* as well as that of the earlier plays I have helped translate with two poets (Sophocles' *Oedipus the King* with Stephen Berg and *Philoctetes* with Carl Philipps).

Now I am left to translate myself, with the help of Andrea Purvis. And in the last leg of this translation Focus Publishing has provided me with a very helpful reader's report, and my series editor (friend and student) Stephen Esposito has helped me as I entered final revisions. He was a student of William Arrowsmith and it seems fitting that he should have the last word—the result of which he is not finally responsible for.

Finally, I acknowledge two further and now remote debts: to T. V. Buttrey, who, in a memorable lecture on *The Trojan Women* given at The Johns Hopkins University, opened my eyes to the meaning of the last scene of the play, as I looked for gods who did not appear on the walls of Troy to save us; and to George Boas, who, during my first years at The Johns Hopkins University, allowed me to read Euripides with him. He was then still a vigorous man in his 80s. We did not read the full text of any of Euripides' plays; only the excerpts from Stobaeus. I recall the pleasure of these readings as I translate Stobaeus for Appendix 1.

The Trojan Women

Dramatis Personae
In order of appearance

Poseidon
Athena
Hecuba
Chorus
of captive Trojan Women
Talthybios
herald of the Greek army, and attendants in non-speaking parts
Kassandra
daughter of Priam
Andromache
widowed wife of Hector and mother of Astyanax
Menelaos
brother of Agamemnon and husband of Helen
Helen
daughter of Leda and Zeus, wife of Menelaos, concubine of Paris
Astyanax
in a non-speaking part

Prologue

Poseidon appears on top of the walls of Troy. He carries his trident. He looks down at the scene below him. Hecuba is rolling in grief before the gates of the city at center stage. Poseidon does not look down on the scene below him until line 36, when he points to Hecuba ("this poor creature"). The stage building displays massive central doors, which represent the gates of Troy. In the foreground on stage are tents housing the women who have not been allotted to the Greek army, but are reserved for the Greek commanders. The walls of Troy are already smoldering. At the end of the play flames will engulf the citadel.

Poseidon
You see me here before you. I am Poseidon.
I have left the salt depths of the Aegean sea, where sea nymphs trace
    the fairest choral dance with their eddying feet.°
From that time when Apollo and I built stone towers° to enclose this
    city
with straight plumb lines, never has affection for this Phrygian city   5
been absent from my heart.
The city now smolders. It has been sacked and destroyed
by the spear of the Argives.
It was Epeios of Phokis° under Parnassos who
inspired by the strategem of Athena,   10
fashioned a horse pregnant with armed soldiers
and sent it within these walls with its cargo of death.
[For this reason men of future generations will call it
the "horse of the wooden spear" for it held within hidden spears.]°
Deserted now are the sacred groves of the gods.°   15
Their great temples drip with blood.
King Priam has fallen at the steps of the altar
of Zeus of the Enclosure;° he lies there dead.

2-3 *the fairest choral dance*: The reference to the ring dances of the Nereids is not
    purely ornamental. It contrasts with the writhing of Hecuba on stage (116, 146-
    52) and her memory of the magnificent dances of the women of Troy during the
    time of its prosperity (333). There is a like contrast in the *Iliad*, when the Nereids
    emerge onto the shore of the Troad to answer Thetis' dirge for Patroklos and
    Achilles, who is now locked in the events that will lead to his death (18.35-51). In
    Homer the sheer music of the names of the Nereids is antiphonal to the grimness
    of human events on the shore of the Troad.

4   *when Apollo and I built stone towers*: According to a Greek legend, reflected in *Iliad*
    21.441 (and in Euripides, *Andromache* 1009 and *Helen* 1511), Apollo and Poseidon
    were forced to serve King Laomedon of Troy for a year, during which time they
    built the walls of Troy.

9   *Epeios of Phokis*: The builder of the Trojan horse. The strategem for finally taking
    Troy is attributed to either Athena or Odysseus — which amounts to the same
    thing.

14-15 These lines are bracketed by most editors as a later marginal and metrical
    addition to explain the obvious. But stating the obvious is a habit in the
    prologues of Euripides.

15 *Deserted now are the sacred groves of the gods*: Poseidon's timely abandonment of
    Troy, the city whose wells he helped build, is the first expression of the grim
    theology of Euripides' *Trojan Women*. Without the human tribute of prayers,
    libations, sacrifice, and festivals, there can be no "honor" (*time*) for the gods.
    Even before Troy's destruction, Athena had abandoned her, as is clear from
    Athena's silent gesture of rejection as the women of Troy bring their offerings to
    her temple on the citadel (*Iliad* 6.311).

18 *Zeus of the enclosure*: This was the Zeus whose altar stood within the enclosure of
    a household. In the Epic Cycle, Priam was slaughtered by Achilles' son, Pyrrhos,
    as he took refuge at the altar of Zeus (cf. *Trojan Women* 481-3 and Figure 3).

Great quantities of gold and plunder from Phrygia
are now being carried down to the ships of the Achaeans. 20
who are waiting for a wind from the east to bring them
in the tenth year of sowing to the longed-for sight
of their wives and children. These are the Greeks
who made the expedition against this city.
I too am leaving fabled Ilion and my altars. 25
I am defeated by Hera,° goddess of Argos, and by Athena,
who together combined to destroy the Phrygians.
When a terrible desolation takes a city,
the world of the gods sickens and will not receive its honors.
The River Scamander echoes the laments of the captured women
who have been assigned by lot° to their owners.
Their new masters are an Arcadian, a Thessalian, 30
and the sons of Theseus° who are the first family of Athens.
The Trojan women who have not been distributed by lot sit there
    below.

> *Poseidon points his trident to their tents below him.*

They have been reserved for the great men of the army.
Among them is Helen, daughter of Tyndareos,
a woman from Laconia, now properly a captive bride. 35

> *Pointing to Hecuba, who is rolling in dirt before the gates of
> Troy and looking at the audience*

And this poor creature, if you can bear to look at her,
lies stretched out before the gates.

---

26 *I am defeated by Hera*: That is, the two goddesses spurned by Paris, Athena and
    Hera, have combined to destroy Troy to avenge the insult of Paris having
    preferred Aphrodite in exchange for Aphrodite's bribe of Helen. The reason for
    their hatred of Troy is alluded to but left unexplained in the *Iliad* (24.22-34; cf.
    3.39 and 13.769). This background is brought explicitly into *The Trojan Women* by
    Hecuba in 924-33.

29 *assigned by lot*: The principle of the division of the human spoils to be led from
    Troy is this: most of the women of the city, including the women who make
    up the chorus, are distributed by lot (*kleros*). But the selection of the most
    important of the captive women has been made by the commanders of the
    army beforehand. Helen, "now properly a captive bride" (35), is reserved for
    Menelaos, although she is from Sparta. Kassandra is reserved for Agamemnon;
    Andromache for the son of Achilles, Pyrrhos (also called Neoptolemos); and
    Hecuba for Odysseus.

31 *the sons of Theseus*: This is the first conspicious symptom of deliberate
    anachronism in the play. In the *Iliad*, the Athenians play an inconsiderable and
    easily forgotten role. Menestheus is mentioned in the Catalogue of Ships (*Iliad*
    2.546-56). In *The Sack of Troy* of the Epic Cycle, Akamas and Demophon play
    some role (*Homeri Opera*, V p. 139 Allen), but the sons of Theseus are important
    to the conception of victors and vanquished articulated in *The Trojan Women*.

Her daughter, Polyxena, has been put to death
at the mound of Achilles' grave, a dreadful death she does
   not know of.   40
The children of Priam and Hecuba are no more.
The daughter Lord Apollo released
in her frenzy, still a virgin,
Agamemnon has "married" by brute force in an adulterous bed,
violating both the god's property and the piety due to him.

   Athena now appears on the walls of Troy.

I have said enough. I say farewell to my city,   45
once fortunate in its dressed stone towers. You would still be
   standing
firm on your foundations, if Athena,
daughter of Zeus, had not destroyed you.

   Athena approaches Poseidon on cue.

Athena
Can I speak to you, a great divinity and a god honored among the
   gods,
who in birth is closest to my father? Can I abandon the enmity that
   has separated us?   50

Poseidon
Lady Athena, you can.
Conversation with kin is a powerful drug over the mind.

Athena
I commend your moderate attitude.
I come to you on matters that concern us both,
   and, my Lord, I will be open with you.

Poseidon
You are not bringing some new announcement from the gods—   55
from Zeus or from another god?

Athena
No. I come on account of Troy, the city on whose walls we stand,
to make a claim on your power.

Poseidon
Can this be? Have you cast aside the hatred
you once had for this city? Have you come to pity it   60
now that it is in ashes?

Athena *Moving along the walls to get a view of the Greek camp*
First, come over here. Can we now speak with one another?
Will you agree to do what I want done?

Poseidon
Indeed, I will. But I would like to know what you have in mind.
Have you come here on account of the Achaeans—or the Phrygians?

Athena
I want to cheer the Trojans, who were once my enemies.   65
I want to inflict upon the Achaean army a bitter home-coming.

Poseidon
Tell me: how can you leap from one emotion to its opposite?
How rapidly you shift from extremes of hate to extremes of love!

Athena
Are you unaware that I and my temples have been outraged?

Poseidon
I am aware of the outrage. I knew of it from the moment Ajax°
    began to drag Kassandra from your altar by force.   70

Athena
And the Achaeans did not lift a finger or utter a word against him!

Poseidon
And yet it was thanks to your power that they sacked Ilion.

Athena
Yes. And with your help I want to do them harm.

Poseidon
I am ready to help you as I can. What do you want me to do?

Athena
I want you to inflict on them a home-coming that will be bitter-
    sweet.   75

---

69   *the moment Ajax began to drag*: This is one of the two crimes committed by the
     Greeks during the sack of Troy that angered Athena especially and turned her
     against them. The other was the removal of her sacred image (*palladion*) from her
     temple on the acropolis of Troy by Odysseus and Diomedes. Both these outrages
     are included in Athena's question to Poseidon: "Are you unaware that I and
     my temples have been outraged?" (69). Poseidon, however, seems to be only
     aware of the case of Kassandra, who had taken refuge at the altar of Athena and
     was dragged from its sanctuary by Ajax, son of Oileus, but in this play at least
     not raped by him. In Arktinos' *The Sack of Troy* the lesser Ajax was destroyed
     by Poseidon for his sacrilege, when he had found safety from shipwreck on the
     Gryai Rocks (the tradition of *Odyssey* 4.499-510).

Poseidon
While they are still on land or upon the salt sea?

Athena
When they have left Ilion and have set sail for home.
Zeus will hurtle down upon them rain and hail unceasing
and sable blasts from the height of heaven.
He promises he will give me the fiery bolt of lightning   80
to strike the Achaeans and burn their ships in a blaze of fire.
Now for your part, Poseidon: Make the sea ways of the Aegean
roar with waves and white caps and swirling water;
choke the Hollow of Euboea° with corpses.
Teach the Achaeans to respect my palaces in the future   85
 and revere the other gods.

Poseidon
This will be accomplished. A favor requires no long argument.
I will roil up the salt expanses of the Aegean Sea;
the capes of Mykonos and the reefs of Delos;°
Skyros and Lemnos and the Kapherean promontories   90
will all receive the corpses of many dead men.
You, Athena, go up to Olympos, take the lightning bolts
from your father's hands, and bide your time.
Wait until the army of the Achaeans is under full sail.
That mortal is a fool who destroys a city,   95
its temples, its tombs, and the precincts of the dead,
making them a waste. He will be destroyed himself.

> *Hecuba has been pitching from side to side in silent grief*
> *before the gates of Troy. She is dressed in black; her gray hair is*
> *unbound and covered with dust and ashes. A group of women*
> *also dressed in black emerge from the entrance to the orchestra*
> *(Parodos) and gather around her. This is the chorus of Trojan*
> *women.*

---

84   *the hollow of Euboea*: This stretch of coast is hard to locate precisely, but the run
     from Troy would take the Greek fleet across the Aegean to Lemnos and Skyros
     and the dangerous Kapherean promontory on the southeast tip of the island of
     Euboea known as the "hollows." This is the cape where the Persian fleet came to
     grief in a sudden squall in the summer of 479 B. C. This storm too was god-sent;
     cf. Herodotus, *The Persian Wars* 8.12-14. It might have figured in the *Palamedes*
     as the coast on which Palamedes' father, Nauplios, engineered the shipwreck of
     some of the returning Greek fleet.

89   *the capes of Mykonos and the reefs of Delos*: according to the epic of *The Returns* (the
     Nostoi of Agias), these rocks (the Gryai) were located off the Cycladic islands of
     Mykonos (where Ajax's grave was shown), Delos, and Tenos.

Hecuba°
Rise up, ill-fated woman. Raise your head
and neck from the ground.
  Troy is no more.

  Turning to the breached and smoldering walls.

This is Troy, and we are the kings of Troy.   100
Hold on as divinity shifts its course.
Our course carries us through the straits.
Some god steers us.
In this disaster I cannot even direct the prow
of my life against the wave.
Aiai! Aiai!   105
Why should I not groan in this inarticulate misery?
Gone are my country, my children, my husband.
O, great billowing glory of my ancestors,
you collapse to this. So you amounted to nothing after all.

  Hecuba remains silent for a time.

Why should I remain silent? Why should I speak out?   110
Why should I raise the cry of lamentation?
I groan over this body
contorted by the weight of some heavy god. I lie stretched out
on my back on this hard bed.
I feel the pain of my head, my temples,   115
my breast.
How I long to roll and toss
and surrender my back and spine to both walls,
like a ship's keel rocking from side to side,
pursuing strain after strain of lamentation and tears.
For the unfortunate even lamentation is a Muse°   120
—to descant misfortunes no chorus can dance to.
You ships' prows

98-152 *Hecuba's Lyric Monologue*: Thematically, Hecuba's language expresses the
    contrast between her present state as she grovels on the ground before the tent
    of Agamemnon and the vanished prosperity of Troy. She conceives of her body
    as a ship driven over a sea churned up by the storm of her misfortunes. The
    metaphorical language with which she describes her body carries forward the
    intimation of the disasters at sea that await Ajax, son of Oileus, and the Achaeans
    (demanded by Athena at 77-78) and Odysseus (forecast by Kassandra in 431-43).

120 *even lamentation is a Muse*: With Hecuba's description of her "Muse" and the
    disasters none can dance to, the chorus of Trojan women enter the orchestra.
    They enter in two groups (half choruses); Hecuba addresses them at line 142. The
    chorus is made up of young women who have lost their husbands in war.

coming to sacred Ilion°
propelled by swift oars over the indigo sea
passing the safe harbors of Greece   125
accompanied by the hateful anthem to Apollo, the Paian,
and the voice of melodious pipes,
you ships' sterns fitted by the plaited
and cultured papyrus of Egypt.°
You came, *ai! ai!*, to Troy's heartland   130
in pursuit of the loathed wife of Menelaos,
the shame of her brother Kastor,
the infamy of the River Eurotas,
the woman who slaughters Priam,
Priam who sowed the seed of fifty children,   135
who slaughters sorrowing Hecuba.
She had run high aground on the beach of this ruin.
oimoi. I groan as I feel this humbled state,
as I lie stretched out next to the tent of Agamemnon.
In my old age I am dragged from my home as a slave.   140
My head bears all the pitiful marks of mourning.
I am a trophy from the sack of Troy.

> *Turning to the chorus who have formed in two groups around*
> *the tent of Agamemnon.*

Enough. You. Pitiful wives of Trojan husbands who were once
armed with bronze swords, daughters ill wed, brides of death.
Join me in my wailing.   145
Troy smolders.
I, a mother,
will lead the piercing keening,
sorrowful as the lament of a feathered bird,
but not as I once did when I had the support of Priam's scepter   150
and led the dance in a stately rhythm
to honor the gods of Phrygia.

---

123 *sacred Ilion*: Like so much of the language of *The Trojan Women*, Hecuba's
     description of the past and the arrival of the Greek fleet on the coast of the Troad
     seems conventional, formulaic, and "poetic." It is symptomatic of the fact that
     poetry and reality have become severely disjointed. Ilion is "sacred" even as it is
     abandoned by its gods.
129 *the plaited and cultured papyrus of Egypt*: a line sometimes daggered and thought
     corrupt because it seems so far-fetched. But much of what Hecuba says *is* far-
     fetched, especially as she describes the vicarious experience of life on board a
     ship in 686-93.

Parodos°

*The two half choruses exchange lyric laments (a kommos) with
Hecuba.*

First Half-Chorus

Strophe A

Hecuba, why do you cry out? What makes you utter these words?
Where has your tale taken us?
We heard the wail of lamentation that pierced our chambers   155
piercing our breasts with fear,
darting dread for the women of Troy.
In these dwellings
  pointing to the tents before the walls
they grieve over their enslavement.

Hecuba

My children, let me answer. Sailors with oars gripped in their hands
are setting off for the ships of the Achaeans.   160

First Half Chorus

Oi 'go! What do they mean to do?
Will they really carry me from my country over the sea?

Hecuba

I do not know. I guess that some disaster is at hand.

First Half Chorus

io, io!
Poor women of Troy, hear now your hard fate.   165
You will be taken from your homes by ship.
The Argives are preparing to return home.

Hecuba   *Responding to a commotion within the tent of Agamemnon*
No! No!
Do not let her come out
wild, frenzied Kassandra, dervish, maenad,   170

_____

153-229 *Parodos* Despite her conception of her threnody for Troy as unsuitable
    for choral dancing, in line 146 Hecuba has begun a choral song (*molpe*) of
    lamentation. She is dressed for the part, in the black garb of woman in mourning
    and with her hair cropped. She is probably wearing what is known as a
    "mourning mask." The women in the two half-choruses that form before her in
    the orchestra are in conspicuous public mourning too.

shame to the Argives.° Do not inflict more pain upon me!
io! io!
Troy, o unhappy Troy. You are no more.
Unhappy are those who leave you,
the living and the dead.   175

Antistrophe B

Second Half Chorus
Oimoi.   My Queen, trembling, in fear, I left this tent
of Agamemnon° to hear what you have to say.
Have the Argives then decided
to put us to death, though we are already wretched?
Or are the sailors standing at the ships' sterns   180
ready to ply their oars?

Hecuba
Children, I have come in fright, my soul
awakened by the gray dawn of terror.

Second Half Chorus
Has a herald from the camp of the Danaans already come?
To whom have I been allotted as a miserable slave?   185

Hecuba
Your lot, I think, is soon to fall.

Second Half Chorus
io! io!
Which Argive, which Thessalian
will take me away? Or will I be taken to some island far from Troy?

Hecuba
Pheu! Pheu!   190
Who will be my master? Where on earth shall I end up
as a slave in my suffering and old age?
A drudge, a crone, the counterfeit of a corpse,
the cold statue of a dead woman.

---

171   *shame to the Argives*: Because of the fact that Ajax, son of Oileus, had attempted
        to rape her and because of the indifference of the Greeks to the sacrilege done to
        Apollo and his priestess at his altar; see the note to line 70.
176-7   *the tent of Agamemnon*: The second choral group has now emerged from the
        tent of Agamemnon in the orchestra, literally the *skene* or tent stretched before
        the walls of Troy. Their song is antiphonal to that of Hecuba and reiterates the
        movement and meter of the strophe. With line 197 the chorus becomes lyrical (in
        meter and in language).

Aiai! Aiai!
Shall I, who was once honored as Queen of Troy,   195
serve as a door keeper or nurse to another's children?

Choral Ode

Chorus

The two half-choruses now join into a single group

Aiai Aiai   What inarticulate sounds
could you summon to grieve over this black day?
Never again will I push the shuttle
along the frame of looms cut from the trees of Mt. Ida.   200
Now for a last time will I look at the home of my parents.
Still greater hardships than this await me.°
I will be forced to share a bed with a Greek—
keep that night and spirit of evil far from me!—
or will I carry water as a pitiable servant
from the sacred stream of Peirene.°   205
Could I have my wish, I would go
to the renowned, blessed,
and prosperous land of Theseus.°
But never would I go to the eddies of the Eurotas,
hateful river that nurtured Helen,°   210
where I would encounter, now a slave,
Menelaos, the sacker of Troy.

Antistrophe B

I have heard rumors of the stately land of Thessaly
watered by the River Peneios,
the fairest approach to high Olympos;   215
I have heard of its fertility, richness, and nodding crops.
After the sacred land of Theseus inhabited by gods

202-29   The chorus now envisage their life in Greece. It is a life Hector had already
predicted for Andromache in his last meeting with his wife (*Iliad* 6.448-61). The
illusion of this choral ode is abruptly shattered by the appearance of Talthybios
at 235, as the chorus conclude that they will be slaves in a Dorian land (234).

205   *Peirene*: an abundant spring in Corinth.

208   *the prosperous land of Theseus*: Attica, a land barely recognized in the Homeric
poems. Athens is mentioned in the Catalogue of Ships (*Iliad* 2.547), but Athenians
play no significant role in either of the Homeric epics.

210   *hateful river that nurtured Helen.* In Greek the Spartan river is qualified as *therapna*.
The place where a cult of Helen was located is also called Therapne, the place of
nurture.

this is the land I would choose.
I have heard of the land
of Mt. Aetna° sacred to Hephaistos,   220
a land that faces the country of the Phoenicians,
the mother to the hills of Sicily;
I have heard of a land proclaimed by the wreathes of victory,
the land that lies closest
to the sailor crossing the Ionian sea,   225
the land watered by the fairest of all rivers,
the Krathis,°
that flows in streams that turn hair to a ruddy hue,
as its divine springs foster
and make prosper this powerful, populous land.

> *As the chorus has been singing their epinician hymn in praise*
> *of Sicily, the herald of the Greek army has entered the stage.*
> *He is accompanied by armed soldiers.*

Now here comes a herald from the army of the Danaans   230
to dispense from his store still new tales.
He comes in a great hurry.
What news is he bringing? What will he tell us?
I know. We are already slaves of a Dorian land.

First Episode°

Talthybios
Hecuba. You know who I am. Woman, I am familiar to you   235
from the many times in the past that I have come to Troy
from the Achaean army.
I am Talthybios. I come with something new to tell.

220-21 *the land of Mt. Aetna*: Sicily. Sicily was of particular interest to Euripides and his
  Athenian audience in the spring of 415, when the Athenians were planning their
  expedition against Syracuse. The language the chorus employ to praise the island
  (not mentioned in the Homeric poems) deliberately recalls the language of the victory odes of Pindar, especially those for the Sicilian victors in the Olympic games.

227 *Krathis*. A river near the city of Sybaris on the instep of Italy flowing into the
  Ionian sea. In 444/3 the site of Sybaris was recolonized by a group led by
  Athenians. The new name of the site was Thurii.

235-510 First Episode ("Kassandra"): Hecuba will remain on stage for the duration
  of *The Trojan Women*; Kassandra's appearance is the first of three scenes in
  which Hecuba and Talthybios confront one of the captive women assigned
  to the leaders of the Greek army. Like her language, the torch she is carrying
  is ambiguous. It is a sign either of her decision to immolate herself or her
  impending "marriage" to Agamemnon. In fact, it is a sign of her impending
  "marriage" to Hades, the bridegroom of young women who die before marriage.
  As is the case of all of the women's parts of this play, her language veers from the
  ecstatic and visionary to the sophistically rational.

Hecuba
This, this, dear women, is what I have long feared.

Talthybios
You have already been allotted to your masters, if this is what you
     feared.   240

Hecuba
Aiai   To what city did you say I am to be taken?
A city of the land of Phthiotis in Thessaly? A city of Kadmos' land?°

Talthybios
Each of you has been allotted to her master; you have not been given
     as a group.

Hecuba
Tell me: Who were the winners in this lottery?
What happy lot awaits the women of Troy?   245

Talthybios
I can tell you, but ask one question at a time, not all at once.

Hecuba
Then tell me:
who was awarded my child, suffering Kassandra?

Talthybios
Lord Agamemnon° chose her from the rest, reserving her for
     himself.

Hecuba
So, to serve as a slave for his Spartan bride.°   250
omoi moi.

Talthybios
No, not a slave, but a "bride" to share his bed in secret.

Hecuba
So, he took the virgin of Phoibos,° the girl the god

---

242 *Kadmos land*: the city of Thebes in Boeotia.

249 *Lord Agamemnon*: In Aeschylus' *Agamemnon*, Agamemnon presents Kassandra to
       Clytemnestra with these words: "This woman before you was my companion,
       the flower picked from many possessions, the gift of my army" (954-5).

250 *his Spartan bride*: Clytemnestra, Helen's half-sister and the daughter of Tyndareos
       and Leda of Sparta.

253 *the virgin of Phoibos*: Apollo granted to Kassandra a life of virginity and the gift of
       prophecy. She is termed virgin twice in *The Trojan Women* (41 and 252; cf. 453).
       But, because she deceived the god of prophecy, he made her prophecies fall on
       deaf—or baffled—ears. This part of her story is briefly told by Kassandra

of the golden locks granted a life that would never know a man's
   bed?

Talthybios
Eros struck him with a barb of passion for the god-frenzied girl. 255

Hecuba   *To Kassandra*
My daughter, throw down those sacred branches!°
Strip from your body this sacred woven dress!

Talthybios
Is it not a great honor for her to attain a king's bed?

Hecuba   *Who pays no attention*
Why have you taken my youngest child° from me?
Where is she?   260

Talthybios
Do you mean Polyxena? or another girl?

Hecuba
Polyxena. To what man was she yoked by her lot?

Talthybios
She has been assigned to serve at Achilles' tomb.

Hecuba
omoi ego.
Did I give birth to a grave attendant?   265
Tell me, my good man:
What Greek custom or ritual is this?

Talthybios
Count your daughter blessed. She is happy.

---

in her exchange with the chorus of Aeschylus, *Agamemnon* 1202-13. But, more
immediately, her gift of prophecy and the disbelief it provoked in Troy was a
feature of the first play of the "trilogy" of which *The Trojan Women* is the third
play; in the *Alexandros* she prophesied the coming of the Greeks to Trojans who
would not believe her.

256   *those sacred branches!* Kassandra is wearing on her head a crown of woolen fillets,
emblems that put her into contact with divinity, and carrying a branch of laurel,
another symbol of her dedication to Apollo. Both are referred to in Aeschylus,
Agamemnon 1265; in *Trojan Women* 330 Kassandra invokes the shrine of Apollo
among the laurels; cf. Euripides, *Andromache* 296.

259   *my youngest child*: Polyxena, Hecuba's youngest daughter, has already been
sacrificed at the gave of Achilles. In the Prologue, Poseidon had announced the
death of Polyxena to Euripides' audience (39-40), but it is only later in the play
that Hecuba registers the force of Talthybios' ambiguous language (622-9). The
same gap in communication occurs in the exchange between Talthybios and
Andromache in 715.

Hecuba
What is the meaning of these words? Tell me:
Does she look upon the light of the sun?   270

Talthybios   *Addressing a woman who does not hear*
She has found her lot in life. She is free of trouble.

Hecuba
And… What of the wife of Hector, the husband who courted her
   with bronze,
poor suffering Andromache? What is her fate?

Talthybios
She too has been reserved. Achilles' son got her.

Hecuba
And I, whom shall I serve,   275
I who must walk with a cane in my shriveled hand?

Talthybios
You were part of the general lottery. You are awarded to Odysseus,°
Lord of Ithaka. You are his slave.

Hecuba
e! e!   This is too much to bear. Strike now your head in mourning
Draw your nails over your cheeks.   280
io moi moi.   Is it then my lot to be the chattel
of an abominable trickster,
an enemy of right, a rabid, lawless beast,
who with his forked tongue
bends everything to its opposite   285
and back again
making what was once hated loved
and what was once loved hated.

   Turning to the chorus

Women of Troy, begin your lament for me.

---

277 *You are awarded to Odysseus*: There seems to be no earlier tradition that Hecuba
   was awarded to Odysseus, although in Euripides' *Hecuba* of 424 Hecuba emerges
   from the tent of Odysseus. In the immediate context of the plays presented at
   the dramatic festivals of 415, Odysseus is the detestable sophist of the *Palamedes*,
   who, in his spite against Palamedes, falsely accused him of treasonable
   correspondence with Priam (Appendix 1). The late fifth-century transformation
   of the Homeric Odysseus into the guileful contemporary sophist explains the
   vehemence of Hecuba's reaction to her fate: the Queen of Troy had become the
   household slave to the archetype of the Athenian demagogue.

I have gone to my evil destiny. I am no more.   290
In my misery I have fallen out as the most unfortunate lot of all.

Chorus
My queen, your lot I know.
But as for our fate, what Achaean, what Greek has power over it?

Talthybios   *To the chorus*
You, serving women, go! It is time to fetch Kassandra.
Be quick! I must entrust her into the general's hands.   295
Then I must bring the women allotted to the others.

    Suddenly turning to the tent of Agamemnon

What is this? Why is a torch blazing inside the tent?
What are the women of Troy doing?
Are they setting their tents afire
because they are about to be taken from Troy   300
to Argos? Do they want to commit suicide by immolating
   themselves?

    To the audience

In a crisis like theirs, the spirit of freedom bends a stiff neck to evils.

    To one of his armed attendants

Open the tent.
I won't have what is good for these women
but hateful to the Achaeans get *me* in trouble.   305

Hecuba
You are wrong. They are not lighting fires. In her divine frenzy
my daughter, Kassandra, is rushing out to us.

Kassandra's lyric monody

Strophe A

    Kassandra has emerged from Agamemnon's tent and holds a
    pine torch out to Hecuba.

Hold this torch!° Take it! Carry the fire! I worship. I burn.
Look! Look here!

---

308 *Hold this torch!* Kassandra rushes out from the tent holding up a torch and sings
    a monody in trochees. The power of this scene derives from her prophecy of her
    coming death and the murder of Agamemnon in Argos, which she will describe
    in grisly detail (448-50). Her true "marriage" is not to Agamemnon, but to Hades,
    in the Greek tradition the bridegroom of young women who died unmarried.

Lord Hymenaeus, this fire is sacred!   310
Blessed is the bridegroom
And blessed I who will be wed to a royal bed
in the land of Argos.
Hymen, Lord Hymenaeus!

> *turning again to Hecuba*

Since you, mother, are lamenting for my dead father   315
and beloved fatherland with ceaseless tears and cries of grief,
I myself will light the flame
to spring to a brilliant shaft of light
at my marriage,
offering it to you, Hymenaeus.   320
offering the torch to you, Hekate,°
to illuminate the marriage bed
of virgins
as custom bids.

Antistrophe A

Let your feet spring into the air,   325
Lead the line of dancers,
euan! euoi! Dionysos, I call on you!
You, mother, are celebrating my father's great blessed fortune!
This is a sacred dance. You, Phoibos,° lead it. I offer sacrifice
in your palace among the laurels.   330
Hymen, O Hymenaeus, Hymen!
Dance, mother, lead the chorus line!
Come join me. Wind your step here with mine.
Dear mother, stop here.

Kassandra deliberately evokes the events of the Greek marriage ceremony, with
its torches to light the way of the bridal procession to the house of the groom,
its invocations to Hymen, the god of marriage, its songs in praise of the bride
and groom (*makarismoi*), and festive dancing. It is only when Kassandra calls
upon the infernal Hekate (323) that the chill of the reality behind her song and
dance invades Euripides' stage. For the Greek audience of this play Kassandra's
invitation to her mother to join her in the wedding dance would have been a
scandal, and the chorus react to it as such (406). Hecuba is in mourning and is not
permitted to join in any festivities. True to her fate, Kassandra is not understood
by the Trojan captives: "Your majesty, will you not stop your daughter?" (342; cf.
407).

321 *Hekate*: a goddess of the underworld, often shown in Greek art as holding a torch.

329 *Phoibos*: Kassandra calls upon both Phoibos Apollo and Dionysos (328). The
two gods, who shared the sacred site of Delphi but who were often viewed as
opposite in character, combine to inspire Kassandra with the exultation of a
Maenad (see 342) and the clairvoyance of a prophet.

Shout out the marriage hymn, Hymenaion, O!   335
with songs of praise
and cries celebrating the bride!

> *To the chorus*

Come now daughters of Phrygians
dressed in your festival gowns, dance, sing the marriage hymn,
sing the groom   340
destined for my bridal bed.

Chorus   *Turning from Kassandra to Hecuba*
Your majesty, will you not stop your daughter? She is possessed by
   a god.
Keep her from whirling in a dance to the camp of the Argives.

Hecuba   *Looking at the torch Kassandra is waving*
Hephaistos, you hold the torch in the weddings of mortal men.
But this flame you ignite gives off a grim light,
something no one would have expected. O, my child, my child,   345
I never thought that you would one day marry like this,
driven at the point of an Argive spear.
Give me the torch. You are not holding it straight,
but dart about like a maenad possessed. Child, your misfortunes
have not taught you any restraint. You have not changed.   350

> *To the chorus*

Women of Troy. Bring the torches on. Let your weeping
be responsive to the wedding songs of this girl.

Kassandra
Mother°, crown my head with the victor's wreath.
Rejoice in my marriage to a king.
Be my escort, and, if my enthusiasm does not match yours,   355
force me to move. If Apollo Loxias is true to his name,°
glorious Agamemnon, great Lord of the Achaeans,
will marry in me a bride more disastrous than Helen.
I will kill him and make him pay for the destruction
of my brothers and father. I shall destroy his house.   360

---

353 Kassandra now reverts to the rhythm of ordinary Greek speech, the iamb (or
     iambic trimeter).
356 *Apollo Loxias*: One of Apollo's epithets is Loxias. It is often associated with Apollo
     as a prophet. It means crooked or oblique and describes the ambiguous character
     of his prophecies.

I say no more. We will not sing of the ax°
that will fall upon my neck and the necks of others;
I will not sing of the struggle of matricides,
a struggle my marriage will bring about; nor of the house of Atreus
   toppled.

    Pointing to the walls of Troy

I shall demonstrate° that this city   365
is more fortunate than are the Achaeans. A god might possess me,
but I shall stand this far distant from his bacchant's dance:
The men who hunted down a single woman and, in Helen, a single
   Kypris
destroyed countless thousands.
That commander, that sage man, lost all that is dearest to him°
for the sake of what is most hateful,   370
surrendering for the sake of his brother the pleasures of children at
   home,
and for the sake of a woman,
a woman who was carried off not by force of violence, but a willing
   partner.
Yet, once they arrived at the banks of the Scamander,
the Achaeans began to die, not for land that had been taken from
   them
or a home or a city with its lofty towers.   375
Those that Ares destroyed never saw their children again;
the hands of their wives did not wrap them in their funeral
   garments.
They lie buried in a foreign land.
Life in Greece mirrors life in Troy.
Wives died off as widows and fathers died after their sons,   380

---

361 *We will not sing of the ax*: as Kassandra did in the prophetic scene in which she
throws open the doors of the palace of Agamemnon to her own death in Aeschylus'
Agamemnon (1256-80); at this moment she also prophesies the revenge of Orestes
and Electra (1280-85). In *The Trojan Women*, unlike the *Oresteia* of Aeschylus,
Kassandra claims that her marriage to Agamemnon, and not Agamemnon's
sacrifice of his daughter, Iphigeneia, will lead inexorably to Agamemnon's murder
by Clytemnestra and reciprocally Clytemnestra's murder by her son.

365 *I shall demonstrate*; Kassandra's "demonstration" is not inspired by her bacchic
and visionary ecstasy, but by the cool calculation of the balance of gains and
losses on both sides of the Trojan War, both of the victors and of the vanquished.

369 *all that is dearest to him*: That is, his daughter, Iphigeneia, whom he sacrificed
to obtain favorable winds for his expedition to Troy from Aulis (the subject of
Euripides' *Iphigeneia at Aulis*). Euripides deflects attention from Agamemnon's
crime of murdering his daughter by using the "apotropaic plural" ("all that is
dearest to him").

having raised children who would never care for them.
There is no one who can bestow at the graves of these men
the gift of a blood-offering to the earth.
The Greek army merits this much praise.
About what is shameful in Greece it is better to keep silent.
I would not have my Muse sing hymns of evil things.°   385
I turn to the Trojans. First, their greatest claim to glory:
they gave their lives for their country.
Those who fell in battle were carried to their homes by their family.
They were covered by the embrace of their native land
and decorously laid out in death by those whose duty it is to bury
   them.   390
Those Phrygians who did not die in battle
lived day by day in the company of their wives and children,
pleasures the Achaeans could not enjoy.

   To Hecuba

Mother, hear the truth about the bitter fate of Hector.
He enjoyed the reputation of being the bravest of men;
   he is now dead and gone.   395
The coming of the Achaeans is responsible for his renown;
had they remained at home, none would have known his worth.
And Paris, he married the daughter of Zeus. Had he not married,
there would have been no word in Troy about this tie of kinship
   with a god.
Anyone with any sense should avoid war.   400
But, if war comes, there is no shame in dying nobly for one's city.
To die as a coward is the crown of infamy.
For these reasons, mother, you should not mourn for our country
or my coming marriage. By this my marriage
I shall destroy those most loathed by you and me.   405

Chorus   *To Kassandra*
What pleasure you take in the disasters of your home!
The burden of this prophetic song will not be as compelling as you
   would have it.

Talthybios   *To Kassandra*
If Apollo had not driven you mad° in Dionysos' frenzy,

---

385   Kassandra's silence powerfully evokes the thought of the wives who have been
         unfaithful to their husbands away in Troy and particularly Agamemnon's wife,
         Clytemnestra, who was seduced by Aigisthos.
408   *If Apollo had not driven you mad*: Again (as in 327 and 329), both Apollo and
         Dionysos are joined as inspiring Kassandra's prophecy.

you would not be sending my commanders off from this land
with such sinister prophecies.   410
So it is: What is exalted and wise in people's esteem
collapses into ashes.
The greatest Lord of the assembled Greek forces,
Atreus' beloved son, has been stricken with a passion for this
      dervish
in preference to all others. I am a poor man,   415
but I would not have chosen this woman for my bed.
You, Kassandra. You are not in your right mind.
I hurl all of your abuse of the Achaeans
and all your praise of the Phrygians to the raging winds.
Follow me now to the ships, a lovely bride for the general.   420

> *To Hecuba*

And you: whenever the son of Laertes wants to take you, follow him.
You will serve a good, prudent woman;°
so say those who come to Ilion.

Kassandra
This man is a clever lackey. How do these men get their titles,
"heralds"?° They are the object of universal detestation among
      mankind.   425
They are mere minions, creatures attached to tyrants and to cities.

> *To Talthybios*

You, do you bring the message that my mother will go
to the halls of Odysseus?

> *Looking away*

What has become, then, of the god Apollo's words?°

422-3   *a good, prudent woman*: Penelope, the wife of Odysseus whose prudence is
        exemplified in her treatment of her suitors and Odysseus in the *Odyssey*, where
        she has the epithet *echephron*, "restrained."

425   *"heralds"*: *kerykes* in Greek. The word is clearly meaningful to Kassandra. One
        explanation of its latent meaning is that Euripides connected it with *ker*, a Greek
        word for the Spirit of Death. It has also been suggested that Talthybios played a
        vile part in the *Palamedes*.

428   *What has become, then, of the god Apollo's words?* In effect, Kassandra is asking:
        "Will the legend of Hecuba and the plot of any *Hecuba* be altered?" Hecuba
        would in fact die in (or near) Troy, but only once she had been transformed into
        a rabid bitch. This transformation occurred after she had avenged the murder
        of her son, Polydoros, by blinding Polymnestor, king of Thrace, and his sons.
        What is too grotesque for Kassandra to utter is the metamorphosis foretold by
        her blinded but seeing victim, Polymnestor: "You will be turned into a rabid
        bitch with a sulphurous mouth, and your tomb will be called Kynosema [Dog's
        Mound] by passing sailors" (Euripides, *Hecuba* 1265-73).

They declare that she will die here. I will not utter the
    shameful part   430
of his prophecy. Unhappy man, Odysseus does not know what
    sufferings await him.
The day will come° when he will look back on my sufferings
and the sufferings of the Phrygians as a golden age.
When he has added ten years to the ten years he has spent here,
    he will arrive at home alone.
He will come first to the narrow passage between cliffs   435
where dread Charybdis dwells. I see the Cyclops,
a mountain cannibal. I see Ligurian° Circe, who transforms men
    into pigs.
I see shipwrecks on the salt sea, the craving for the lotus,
the sacred cattle of the Sun God, whose bleeding flesh
will one day sing a bitter song that will make Odysseus'
    flesh crawl.   440
I will cut my story short. Still living, he will enter Hades,
and, once he has survived shipwreck at sea,
he will discover countless troubles on his return home.
But, ... why should I harp on the hardships of Odysseus?

> *Turning to Talthybios again*

Get on your way. Join our bridegroom in the Halls of Hades.   445
That coward will be given a coward's burial, at night, not in the light
    of day.
You, commander of Danaids not Danaans, of women not men,
you fancy that you are accomplishing some magnificent feat.
And I—my corpse—cast down naked, the deep ravines,
as they run in winter torrent, will yield up to beasts to share,
near the tomb of my groom, I, Apollo's priestess.   450

> *Kassandra takes the strands of wool that have bound her hair*
> *and throws them to the ground.*

---

432 *The day will come*: A prophecy inspired and confirmed by Odysseus' words (in
     Odyssey 5.306-7), as he recalls the prophecy of Kalypso, as a storm overtakes his
     raft within sight of the island of Skeria (5.206-7):

> Happy, thrice happy, and four times happy are the Danaans
> who died then in the broad plains of Troy, as they sought to please
> the sons of Atreus.

   In her prophecy of the sufferings of Odysseus, Kassandra abbreviates Homer's
   account of Odysseus' return to Ithaka after twenty years; she completely neglects
   his stay in Phaeacia and the Phaeacians' recognition of the valor of Odysseus,
   and she ignores his final reunion with his family and his triumph in Ithaka.

437 *Ligurian*: on the northwest coast of Italy.

Wool fillets sacred to the god who is dearest to me,
lovely proud emblems of my bacchanals,
I leave you. I am done with the festivals in which I once exulted.
Leave me, I tear you from my body, while my body is still undefiled.
Let the winds, Apollo, god of prophecy, carry them back to you.

> *To Talthybios*

Where is the general's ship? Which ship must I board?   455
You need not wait for a breeze to fill the sails.
In me you are transporting from this land a Fury,
    a single avenger of three crimes.°

> *To Hecuba*

Mother, do not say good-bye. Beloved country,
brothers beneath its soil, father who sired us,
in a short time you will greet me. I shall arrive among the dead,   460
a victor, when I have destroyed the Atreidai, who have destroyed us.

Leader of the Chorus   *To some of the chorus*
You who watch over old Hecuba, can't you see
how your mistress has collapsed without uttering a sound?
Will you not help her up? Cowardly women,
will you leave the old woman on the ground? Lift her up.   465

Hecuba
Leave me, girls. Leave me where I have fallen.
There is no love in help when I don't want it.
For what I am suffering, have suffered, and have still to suffer,
I have the right to fall.

> *Looking up*

Gods!° I call upon craven allies. Even so, there is a kind
    of propriety   470
in calling on you, when one of us mortals meets misfortune.

> *She gets to her feet*

First, now: It is my pleasure to sing of our blessings,

---

457   *a single avenger of three crimes*: Euripides is not being learnedly precise here and
      making Kassandra one of the three Furies (Erinyes). Kassandra sees herself
      rather as avenging three deaths: those of her father, her brothers, and Troy; cf.
      359-60 and 461.

470   *Gods!* Hecuba's appeal to the gods has its parallel in Thucydides' history of the
      Peloponnesian war in the vain appeal to the gods by the desperate people of
      Melos (5.104) and Nikias' exhortation to the commanders of his fleet to pray
      to the gods just before the final Athenian defeat in Sicily (7.69.2). The gods
      responded to the appeals of neither the Melians nor the Athenians.

for by their contrast I will impart a more tragic strain to our
    disasters.
Yes, I was born to royalty and destined to it.
As Queen, I gave birth to children who excelled all others,   475
and not in their mere number did they stand above all other
    Phrygians.
No mother, Trojan, Greek, or barbarian
could ever boast as do I over my sons.
These sons I saw fall under the arms of the Greeks.
Over their graves I cropped this head in mourning.   480
I wept for Priam, who sired them. No one had to tell me of his death;
I witnessed it with these eyes,

> *Touching her lacerated cheeks*

butchered a suppliant at the altar of our hearth.
And I saw Troy captured. The daughters I brought up
to be the choice brides of the most eligible suitors   485
were raised for other husbands, snatched from my hands.
There is no hope they will ever see me again
or that I will ever again set eyes upon them.
As for the rest of my life's story, the miserable conclusion is this:
I shall arrive in Greece in old age as a slave.   490
My masters will assign me tasks that are not at all fitting
to a woman of my age: to hold keys
as a door-keeper, I, the mother of Hector!
to grind meal and sleep with my back on a hard floor
and ache. I am an old woman, used to the bed of a king.   495
My body will be covered with rags that were once fine robes,
a disgrace for people who were once well to do.
oi 'go talaina   I am so miserable.
The wedding of one woman has caused all this and will continue to
    cause more grief.

> *Turning to Kassandra*

Child, maenad dancing wildly with the gods,   500
what catastrophes have loosened the belt of your purity?

> *Looking away*

And you, my poor girl, Polyxena, where are you?
Of all the children of this fruitful womb
what son or daughter is here now to help me?

> *Hecuba slumps to the ground and is helped up again by*
> *members of the chorus.*

Why are you helping me up?   505
What can move you to do so?
Lead me in the dance, lead my foot once so delicate in Troy,
now that I am a slave lead me to a straw bed on a dirt floor
with a stone pillow for my queen's tiara. I am fallen.
Women, count no mortal—man or woman—happy° before death
   arrives.   510

Chorus
   Stasimon A°
   Strophe
Muse, sing for me the song of Ilion.
Sing a tearful hymn
of lamentation for the dead;
sing in a new strain.
Now I will sing out to echoing Troy   515
and tell how I was destroyed
and endured capture at spear point
and from the four-wheeled
carriage of the Argives,
when the Achaeans left the horse whose rumble reached high
   heaven   520
as it rolled with its rattling cargo of arms,
and its golden cheek-piece glittered.
The people of Troy shouted to heaven:
"Go out now, you men who are now at the end of your suffering,
draw this sacred wooden image   525

---

510   *count no mortal ... happy*: The word in Greek is *eudaimon*. This warning, familiar
      as it is in tragedy, is most familiar as Solon articulates it in his interview with
      King Croesus of Lydia (in Herodotus, *Histories* 1.32). It is fitting that Euripides
      should give these words to an oriental queen, who speaks of herself and Priam as
      "tyrants" (474) and recalls her past prosperity by recalling the Herodotean word
      olbios ("blessed," or "prosperous," 497). *Eudaimon*, by contrast, involves the favor
      of the gods.
511-67 Stasimon A ("The Fall of Troy") This is the first full choral song of *The
      Trojan Women*. The chorus has joined as a whole to perform it. In their entry
      song (*parodos*) the chorus had divided into two groups and their singing was
      antiphonal to Hecuba's lamentation. This lamentation (*kommos*) carries over into
      this song, which they begin by asking the Muse to sing in a "new strain" (514).
      The invocation is epic and recalls the opening invocations of both the *Iliad* and
      Odyssey (and in the dactylic meter of the epic) and it commemorates a moment in
      the Trojan War beyond the narrow range of the *Iliad* (but not the *Odyssey*)—the
      moment that seemed to mark the triumph of the Trojans in their defensive war of
      ten years.

up to the virgin goddess of Ilion,° daughter of Zeus."
Was there a young woman who did not go out into the streets?
Was there an old man who did not leave his home?
They all felt joy in their festive songs,
and in their delusion they bent under slavery's yoke.   530

Antistrophe

The entire nation of Phrygia
rushed to the gates
to the horse of mountain pine,
to the wood-crafted ambush of the Argives,
in their eagerness to offer this bane to the goddess of Dardanos'
    land,   535
a thanks offering to the unyoked goddess of the immortal foals.°
With ropes of plaited flax they drew it,
like some black ship,° soon to stain their country with blood,
to the stone seat
and foundation of Pallas Athena,   540
The dark of night settled
on their labor and joy;
the lotus wood pipes of Libya throbbed out
tremulous Phrygian airs,
and the young women responded to   545
their rhythm with the beat of their feet.
and lifted their festal song.
But in their homes
fierce tongues of fire
gave a black glint to sleep.   550

---

526 *the virgin goddess of Ilion*: Athena. The blindness of the seemingly triumphant and
     truly pious Trojans is well exhibited in their response to this gift of a wooden
     horse. In Euripides' play there is no Laokoon to question or Helen to test this
     "gift" to Athena.
536 *the unyoked goddess of the immortal foals*: in Greek cult, the virgin goddess (thus
     "unyoked") Athena, bore the epithets *Hippia* and *Chalinitis*, "Goddess of the
     Horse," "Goddess of the Bridle." It is clear from the *Iliad* and the scene in which
     the women of Troy, led by Hecuba, supplicate Athena in her temple on the
     acropolis of Troy that she has turned her face against Troy (*Iliad* 6.286-312).
538 *like some black ship*: The comparison is not idle, but it could not belong to the
     actual experience of Euripides' chorus of Trojan women. It belongs rather to the
     experience of Euripides' Athenian audience seated in the theater of Dionysos.
     Every four years, during the Panathenaia, a cloak woven for the statue of Athena
     was hoisted on the mast of a ship that was drawn up to the acropolis.

Epode

I for my part danced in a chorus° within my chambers
and was singing the mountain-ranging daughter of Zeus,
when a blood-curdling shout
crested over
the high battlements of Troy.   555
Babes in arms
clutched with hands
trembling with terror
the robes of their mothers,
and Ares began to emerge from ambush   560
in the horse that was the work of virgin Pallas.°
There was slaughter about the altars of the sanctuary.
The cropped hair,°
the desolation of young widows,
carried a wreath of fertility   565
to Greece and her young,
but black mourning for the country of the Phrygians.

---

551   *I for my part danced in a chorus*: It is significant that the women singing this choral
      ode speak of others as dragging the offering of the wooden horse up to the
      temple of Athena and of still other unmarried women as performing nocturnal
      choral dances in her honor to the accompaniment of a flute (543). The chorus
      honor another daughter of Zeus, Artemis ("the mountain-ranging daughter of
      Zeus," 551), a goddess who in the *Iliad* favored the Trojans and, unlike Athena,
      did not turn against her votaries. In this way, the chorus appear to disassociate
      themselves from Athena.

561   *the work of virgin Pallas*: the author of the strategy of building the Trojan horse
      was Odysseus; the builder Epeios of Phokis (cf. 9-10). But clearly Odysseus'
      cunning owes something to Athena, who is here held responsible for his
      strategem and the destruction of Troy.

563   *cropped hair*: Euripides' conceit is difficult because it violently combines two
      points of view. From one point of view, that of the Trojans, the emptiness of
      the beds of the Trojan widows is paired with the cutting of their hair as a sign
      of mourning (as in Sophocles, *Electra* 52). But, from another point of view, the
      desolation of captive women forever separated from their husbands bears the
      victor's crown to the Greeks. This "crown," symbolized by the close cropped hair
      of the captive women, can be described as "a wreath of fertility," because these
      slaves will bear new sons to their masters, as did Andromache to Neoptolemos
      (Euripides, *Andromache* 24-5).

Second Episode°

A wagon has entered the orchestra. It carries Andromache,
her young son, Astyanax, and spoils taken from Troy.
Andromache is dressed in black, her hair cropped as a sign of
public mourning for her husband, Hector.

The chorus to Hecuba

Hecuba, can you see Andromache° being transported in this foreign
    cart?
Little Astyanax,
Hector's son,   570
rocks to the heaving motion of his mother's breasts.

    To Andromache

Unlucky woman, where are they taking you away from Troy,
mounted on this carriage with Hector's armor
and the spoils of Phrygia
that are the prizes of the hunt in war.
These trophies the son of Achilles   575
will hang on the temples of Phthia.

    Andromache and Hecuba begin an antiphonal song of
    lamentation (kommos).

568-798 Second Epode ("Andromache"). This is the middle episode of this episodic
    play. It is the scene that focuses most sharply on the fate of the women taken
    captive by the victorious Greek army. Hector had foreseen the life Andromache
    would lead once he had fallen and she had been taken away from Troy as a
    slave (*Iliad* 6.448-63), but he could not have foreseen the "hostage syndrome" by
    which Andromache would become reconciled to her new husband, Achilles' son,
    Neoptolemos. Nor could he foresee Andromache's fate as a slave to a woman
    like Menelaos' daughter, Hermione, the subject of Euripides' *Andromache*, written
    perhaps a decade before the production of the *Trojan Women*.

568 *can you see Andromache?* Andromache has entered the stage platform from the
    parodos (to the right of the audience, indicating that she has come from the city)
    carried on a cart on which she and her son, Astyanax, are being transported with
    other loot taken from Troy. Euripides has staged this scene to recall the entry
    of Kassandra in Aeschylus' *Agamemnon* (906 and 1039) and he has deliberately
    substituted Kassandra's carriage (*apene*) for a cart (*okhos*). Andromache's entry
    into the theater conveys in simple visual terms the meaning of the Greek
    expression for plundering—"carrying and leading." The victorious army would
    carry its plunder away and lead off domestic animals, women, and children.

Stophe A

Andromache
My masters, the Achaeans, are taking me away.

Hecuba
Oimoi.

Andromache
    Why do you groan this hymn of my triumph?°

Hecuba
Aiai

Andromache
    You groan for our pain.

Hecuba
O Zeus!

Andromache
    You groan for our ruin.   580

Hecuba
My children!

Andromache
    We were once your children.

Antistrophe A

Hecuba
Gone is our good fortune, gone is Troy.

Andromache
Poor, poor woman.

Hecuba
    Gone the noble ancestry of our children.

Andromache
Pheu Pheu

---

578 *Why do you groan this hymn of my triumph?* Euripides' language is difficult once
again because of the sudden and violent shift in the point of view (see the note to
564). To the ears of the Greek conquerors, Hecuba's anguished *oimoi* is the sound
of a paean of triumph; to the ears of the Trojans the sound of the flutes that
accompanied the landing of the Greeks on the coast of the Troad is a "hateful
paean" (126). The ambiguity of perspective goes back to Aeschylus, *Agamemnon*
715, where the chorus describe the groans of captured Troy as a "dirge-filled
paean" (as I would emend the text).

Hecuba
   Pheu Lament then my

Andromache
evils.

Hecuba
  Our heart-breaking fate.   585

Andromache
Grieve for our city.

Hecuba
     A city now smoldering.

Strophe B

Andromache
My husband, come to me.

Hecuba
You call out to my son, poor woman.
He is in Hades.

Andromache
Come, protect your wife.   590

Antistrophe B

Andromache
I call on you, once the curse of the Achaeans

Hecuba
I call on you, ancient Priam,
Lord of our children.

Andromache
Take me into the halls of Hades.

Strophe C

Andromache
Mine is a deep longing.

Hecuba
     You are adamant. *We* feel these pains. 595

Andromache
Pain for a city that is no more.

Hecuba
        Pain heaped on pain.

Andromache
Pain caused by the hostility of the gods from the time when your
  son escaped Hades°
the son who, for an abominable marriage, destroyed the citadel of
  Troy.
Now bodies of the dead lie exposed at the temple of divine Pallas.
Vultures will pick their bones. Athena has put Troy under slavery's
  yoke.   600

 Antistrophe

Hecuba
Troy, my desolate land!

Andromache
       You are abandoned. I weep for you.

Hecuba *Pointing to the walls of Troy*
Now you can see its tragic end.

Andromache
       You can see the house where I gave birth.

Hecuba
My children. Your mother, who has lost her city, is now abandoned
  by you.
Tears drip down in an unending stream,   605
shrill is the mourning for our houses destroyed! The dead are dead
  to our pain.

Chorus
Yes, tears are sweet to those in trouble
and the heart-rending strain of lamentation and the Muse of
  suffering.

Andromache *Calling attention to herself and her son in the wagon*
Mother of the hero Hector, who killed more Argives than any other
  Trojan,   610
do you see these spoils of war?

---

597 *from the time when your son escaped Hades*: When she was pregnant with Paris,
  Hecuba had a dream that she had given birth to a firebrand. Priam's decision to
  expose Paris, rather than incurring the pollution of killing him, and his rescue
  from death explain his "escape from Hades." This matter was taken up in the
  Prologue of the *Alexandros* (for which see Appendix 1).

Hecuba

What I see is the work of the gods. They raise up to towering heights
what was once nothing. What seems to tower above us do they
   destroy.

Andromache

I and my son are being carried off as plunder;
Subject to these laws of change, nobility has been reduced
   to slavery,   615

Hecuba

Force is the most terrible thing about necessity. Kassandra has just
   gone from me,
dragged away by brute force.

Andromache

Pheu Pheu
So it seems that another was Ajax to your daughter.°
But your sickness spreads still farther.

Hecuba

There is no end to my sickness, no term.   620
One disaster comes to vie with another.

Andromache

Your daughter Polyxena is dead. She was slaughtered,
a victim at the grave of Achilles, an offering to a lifeless corpse.

Hecuba

Oi 'go   So this is the clear meaning of those riddling words
Talthybios spoke so darkly.   625

Andromache

I saw her body myself. I got down from the wagon,
covered her with a robe, and mourned over her body.

Hecuba

Ai Ai   Child, child! You were the first victim of their abominable
   rites!
Ai Ai   I cry out in pain for your terrible death.

Andromache

She died as she died. Even so, her fate   630
was kinder than mine. I must go on living.

---

618 *another was Ajax to your daughter*: Agamemnon, that is, who will follow Ajax, son
    of Oileus, in his violation of Kassandra. See the note to line 70.

Hecuba
To see the light of day is not the same as death.
Death is nothing. In life hope still lives.

Andromache
[Mother, you who gave birth to Polyxena, Listen to me.
I have an excellent argument. I want to give your heart
    some joy.]   635
I say that never to have been born is the same as being dead.
It is better to be dead than to live a life of distress.
The dead are done with suffering and feel absolutely no pain;
but the person who has experienced good fortune
and falls into ill fortune is distraught at the thought of lost
    happiness.   640
Polyxena is now dead. It is as if she had never seen the light of day.
She knows nothing of the evils that have befallen her.
But I, I who set my sights on the target of a good reputation,
who had my share of the goods of Fortune, I missed my mark.
For all those qualities that are found admirable in a woman°   645
were the object of my constant striving when I lived under
    Hector's roof.
First and foremost: I kept inside the house.
Whether or not there exists real cause for gossip,
the woman who does not stay indoors attracts a bad reputation
simply by going out. I gave up all longing for the world
    outdoors   650
and did not admit into my chambers the sophisticated talk of
    women.
My native good sense tutored me; I did not need the company of
    other women.
Rumor of these excellent qualities reached the Achaean camp and
    destroyed me.
When it came to the distribution of the women set apart,
the son of Achilles chose me as his wife.
I will live as a slave in the house of murderers.   660

---

645 *all those qualities that are found admirable in a woman*: The Greek word for these
    admirable qualities is *sophrosyne* ("prudent restraint"). This is an expression of
    the male ideal of a virtuous wife and, like many other gnomic passages scattered
    throughout Euripidean tragedy, it helps establish Euripides' reputation as
    a misogynist. The "ideal" Andromache is holding up for her mother-in-law
    articulates a system of contrasts. Women are kept indoors and are expected to
    maintain a modest silence and exercise complaisance before their husbands.
    Their husbands, by contrast, enter their houses fresh from a world of speech and
    action outdoors, both in the assembly and on the battlefield.

If I thrust from me the beloved head of Hector°
and open my heart to my present husband,
people will think that I am a traitor to my husband.
But, if I loathe my new husband, my masters will hate me.
And yet... they say that a single night   665
melts a woman's resistance to a man's bed.
I scorn the woman who rejects her former husband
for the bed and love of another.
There is no filly who will easily pull the yoke
when separated from the filly she has been reared with.   670
Yet a brute beast is born with no language.
Having no intelligence a beast is inferior to human beings.

> *Turning away from Hecuba*

In you, Hector, I had the husband I wanted.
You were great in intelligence, nobility, wealth, and courage.
When you took me from my father's house° I knew no man.   675
You were the first to yoke me as a bride to your bed.
Now, Hector, you are gone. But I will be carried as a captive of war
on a ship to Greece and the yoke of slavery.

> *Addressing Hecuba*

Does not, then, Polyxena's death, which you lament so grievously,
hold fewer evils than my life?   680
I do not even have hope as my companion,
hope, the companion of all other mortals.
I am not deluded. I am set on no noble course. But it is sweet to
    think so.

Chorus
You have reached the same depth of misfortune as have I.
In your lamentation you have taught me the extent of my
    own pain.   685

Hecuba
I have never set foot on a ship, but I know ships:
I have seen paintings of them and I have heard about them.

---

661 *the beloved head of Hector*: it was the custom for the wife to cradle the head of her
     dead husband in the rituals of public mourning, a scene often shown in Greek
     vase painting.
675 *when you took me from my father's house*: In her last meeting with Hector,
     Andromache recalls how Hector took her from the house of Eetion and speaks in
     dread of her desolation if Hector should die. Achilles had killed her father and
     sacked her city. All she has left is her husband, Hector (*Iliad* 6.410-30).

If sailors enjoy moderate weather
they are confident that they will escape difficulties.
One is stationed at the rudder; another at the mast;   690
and another mans the bilge pump. But if a heavy sea
should rage and break over the ship, the crew
surrenders itself to Fortune and commits itself to the running of the
    waves.
Such a sailor am I. Many are my troubles.
I cannot utter a word. I surrender my power of speech.   695
The disastrous surge of a god-sent storm overwhelms me.

> *Turning to Andromache*

Enough of that. My dear child,
do not dwell overmuch on Hector's fate. Your tears cannot save him
    now.
Rather, show respect to your present master and owner.
Dangle before him the lure and charm of your good behavior.   700
If you do as I say, you will bring comfort to all your loved ones
and you will, perhaps, one day raise this boy,

> *Pointing to Astyanax*

son of my son,
to be the salvation of Troy. Sons of your sons
will found Ilion once again,
and once again Troy will become a city.   705

> *Talthybios and his attendants approach.*

One thought begets another.
What do I see here? Is the Achaeans' lackey
coming to proclaim still new decisions?

Talthybios   *Keeping at a safe distance from Andromache*
Andromache. You are the wife of the man who was once the most
    heroic of the Phrygians.
Do not hate me for what I have to say. It is not my choice   710
to bring messages from the Danaans and the family of Pelops.

Andromache
What is the message? This is a prelude to some evil tale.

Talthybios
The army has voted that this boy...How can I say it?

Andromache
No! He won't be the slave of another master than mine?

Talthybios
No Achaean will ever be his master.°   715

Andromache
Then will they leave him in Troy as the last remnant of the
    Phrygians?

Talthybios
I know of no good way to tell you evil.

Andromache
I respect your decent hesitation—unless what you have to say is evil.

Talthybios
To tell you the evil truth: they mean to kill your son.

Andromache
Oimoi
These words are an evil greater than what you said about my
    marriage.   720

Talthybios
Odysseus prevailed in a speech before the Greek assembly. He
    said…

Andromache
Ai Ai mal'   There is no end to the evil we suffer.

Talthybios
… he said that we should not let the son of a heroic father grow to
    manhood.

Andromache
I wish he would prevail on the army to sentence his own son to the
    same fate!

Talthybios   *Still not responding to Andromache*
The decision was that he must be thrown from Troy's towers.   725
Andromache, let this be. Be wise and accept it.

        Andromache reaches to Astyanax and holds him tight

Do not cling to the boy. Bear the pain of your adversity with nobility.
Do not think that you have any power when you have no strength.
You have no one to protect you. Consider, as you must:

---

715 *No Achaean will ever be his master*: Again, Talthybios' words are ambiguous and
       misunderstood, as was the case when he spoke to Hecuba of the fate of Polyxena
       in 260-71.

you have lost your city and your husband.   730
You are now under our control.
For these reasons do not be eager for combat.
Do nothing that would bring disgrace or resentment upon you.
And I will not have you hurl curses upon the Achaeans.
If you utter a word to enrage the army,   735
your son will receive no burial, none of the rites of mourning
     for the dead.
But, if you keep quiet and manage your misfortunes as best you can,
it is just possible that you will not leave this boy unburied
and that you yourself might find the Achaeans better disposed to
     you.

Andromache   *Turning to Astyanax*
O, my dearest child, my greatest treasure,   740
you will die at the hands of enemies, leaving your mother to her
     sorrows.
The noble birth of your father has been the cause of your undoing;
for others this nobility proved their salvation.°
Your father's nobility came too early for you.
My nuptials and my marriage were doomed,   745
doomed the house of Hector, which I entered as a bride,
with no thought that the son I bore would become a victim of the
     Danaans.
I thought he would be monarch over all of fertile Asia.
My child, you are weeping. Do you sense your misfortunes?
Why are you clinging to me, holding onto my robe.   750
like a baby bird quivering under its mother's wings?
Hector will not rise up from beneath the earth
and come, gripping his spear, to save you.
You have no protection in your father's family or the might of the
     Phrygians.
You will hurtle pitiably from the heights in a dead plunge   755
and break your neck. Your soul will break out from your body.
Let me embrace your dear, young body, and smell your skin's sweet
     breath.
So, ... all my hopes were vain.
This breast nursed you when you were a babe in swaddling clothes.
All my care, all the labor that wore me out were for nothing.   760

742-3   These lines are bracketed in Diggle's Oxford edition. Possibly, they are an
         actor's interpolation. But the thought is worth considering: Astyanax was feared
         by the Achaeans because they believed that he would inherit his father's valor
         (cf. Euripides, *The Sons of Herakles* 468-70).

Now put your arms around your mother, give me a last hug.
Come to the mother who gave you life.
Wrap your arms around me. Kiss me, child.
You civilized Greeks! With your evil, barbaric inventions!
Why kill this boy? He did nothing to you!   765
And you, daughter of Tyndareos, you were never the daughter of
    Zeus!°
I say that you are the spawn of many fathers:
Avenger first, then Spite,
Gore, and Blood, and Death. All the crop of evil Earth yields begot
    you!
I will never take pride in claiming that Zeus was your father.   770
For many a Greek and many a barbarian you are the black Death
    Spirit!
I wish you dead! The gleaming light of your lovely eyes
has destroyed in ugly fashion the famous plains of Troy.

> *To Talthybios*

Now, go: drive off your plunder! Carry it away with you! Throw it
    down!
If this is your decision.
Feast on this child's flesh. The gods, I know, will our utter
    destruction,   775
and we Trojans could never shelter him from death.
Cover this tormented body and throw it into the ship.
I am headed for a splendid wedding celebration,
now that I have lost my child.

Chorus
Poor, suffering Troy! Because of a single woman and a loathsome
    marriage   780
you have lost countless thousands.

> *Talthybios and his men approach Astyanax.*

---

766 *you were never the daughter of Zeus*: Andromache regards Helen rather as the
    daughter of the mortal Tyndareos. Helen resembles the hero Herakles in that
    she can be regarded as the child of either a divine or mortal father. Herakles
    was the son either of Zeus and Alkmene or of Amphitryon and Alkmene; Helen
    the daughter either of Zeus and Leda or of Tyndareos and Leda. Andromache
    addresses Helen by the name of her mortal father and then the abstractions
    she embodies. These abstractions reveal the tradition that Helen had another
    immortal mother, Nemesis, the goddess of resentment and retribution ("Avenger
    first"). But she can also be called "daughter of Zeus" (*Dios kore*), just as her
    brothers are known as the sons of Zeus (*Dioskouroi*; cf. 398 and 1109).

Talthybios
Come, son. Leave the arms of your sorrowful mother
and mount to the towers of your ancestors,
the crown of your city.
There it is decreed that you shall breathe your last.   785

> *To his attendants*

Take him away. It is the duty
of a better friend than am I
to our shameful decision
to make proclamations such as this.

Hecuba
Child, son of my sad son,   790
your life is being snatched from us
unjustly, robbed from your mother and myself.
What will become of me? What can I do for you, doomed child?

> *Hecuba settles into a mourning position.*

We can give you these gestures of mourning as we beat our head
    and breasts.
Of mourning and lamentation we are masters. *oi 'go.*   795
I cry out for our city; I cry out for you.
What do we now lack? What more do we need
to drive us into utter destruction?

> *Talthybios and his attendants lead Astyanax off stage right.*
> *Andromache returns to her wagon.*

Chorus

Second Stasimon°
Strophe A

O, Telamon, king of Salamis, land flowering with bees,
you established your home and seat   800
on an island washed by beating waves
facing the sacred slope

799-859 Second Stasimon ("Ganymede"): The chorus look back. In the generation
    before the Trojan War, Telamon (brother of Peleus and father of Ajax, king of the
    island of Salamis) joined Herakles and Philoctetes in the first Greek assault on the
    Troy of King Laomedon, father of Priam. As a reward for his efforts, he received
    Hesione, daughter of Laomedon, as a slave. The chorus also move back to a time
    when the gods were joined to Troy: Zeus in his passion for the Trojan Ganymede
    and the goddess of the dawn (Eos) in her passion for the Trojan Tithonos. But
    Troy holds no more charms for the gods (858-9).

where Athena first revealed the sprig of the olive,° green and gray,
a celestial crown and jewel for bright, prosperous Athens.
Salamis, you left, you left, with the archer son of Alkmene   805
to share in noble exploits
for Ilion, for Ilion, to destroy our city, what was once our city,
when you came from Greece,

Antistrophe A

When Herakles first led the flower of Greece,
dishonored as he was over the broken promise of the horses,°
he brought ships that cleave the sea   810
to rest at the gliding current of the Simois,°
and tied them prow up to the shore.
He took from his ships
a cargo of arrows sure of their mark
to carry death to Laomedon.
Then he razed the walls built straight to Apollo's plumb
     and rule   815
with a crimson blast of fire,
and destroyed the land of Troy.°
Twice, in twin strokes
around Troy's walls, did a lance stained with blood
overthrow the walls of Dardanos.

---

803 *where Athena first revealed the sprig of the olive*: Euripides sets Athena's revelation
     of the olive to mankind in the tradition of another gift of a goddess to mankind.
     In neighboring Eleusis, Demeter "revealed" the crops of grain to mortals and
     initiated them into her rites (in the language of the Homeric *Hymn to Demeter* 474;
     cf. Euripides, *Ion* 1434). The olive tree that was thought to have been planted by
     Athena was burned in the Persian sack of the acropolis in 480, but the next day it
     miraculously sprouted a new shoot (Herodotus, *Histories* 8.55).

809 *the broken promise of the horses*: Laomedon promised Herakles divine horses if
     he would rescue his daughter Hesione from a sea-serpent. Herakles kept his
     engagement, but Laomedon did not. Thus, the first Trojan War.

811 *Simois*: With the Scamander, one of the two rivers of the Troad. In the tradition of
     the Argonauts, it was conceived of as the port of Troy

817 The text is disputed. Diggle's emendation of "the descendants of Dardanus"
     (*Dardanidas*) for "the land of Dardanos"(*Dardanias*) is tempting; it makes the
     descendants of Zeus the victims of two wars and prepares the way for the
     reflections of the chorus on the gods' utter lack of concern for the humans whom
     their passions and rancor involve them with. But the context calls attention to the
     walls and therefore the land of Troy.

Strophe B

So it is. Ganymede,° Laomedon's son, you step daintily now   820
among the golden cups, pouring wine,
filling the cup of Zeus, a noble service,
but for nothing.
The city of your birth is ablaze.   825
The cliffs
at the sea's edge
cry out the shrill cry
of a sea bird
that has lost her young,   830
their echo eddies along the shore,
the lament for a marriage lost
for children, for old mothers.
Gone now are the fresh pools where once you bathed
and the running courses of the gymnasia.   835
But you, Ganymede, now thrive beside
the throne of Zeus.
Peace, and light and the calm of the sea
radiate from your young face.
But below Greek spears have destroyed the land of Priam.   840

Antistrophe B

Eros, god of passion, once you came
to the halls of King Dardanos.
The eyes of the goddesses of heaven were upon you.
How high did you then make Troy tower,
as you joined Troy in kinship° with the gods?   845
But I will say nothing in dispraise of Zeus.°

---

820 *Ganymede*: in Euripides' genealogy, Ganymede was the son of Laomedon; in
     another genealogy, he was the son of Tros (*Iliad* 5.265-6). He stirred the passion of
     Zeus. To possess him Zeus transformed himself into an eagle and carried him up
     to heaven, where he served as the cup-bearer of Zeus and the other immortals.

845 *kinship*: The putative bond created between immortal and mortal is termed a
     kedos, a bond that for humans is created by marriage. It establishes a mutual
     concern between two groups that are not related by blood. Thus, the word can
     also mean mourning, just as the Greek word for a mother-in-law comes from
     penthos, mourning. The *penthera* is a woman for whom one must mourn.

846 *But I will say nothing in dispraise of Zeus*: The chorus recognize that they cannot
     speak frankly of the erotic bond between Zeus and the young Trojan Ganymede
     as a *kedos* (see note to line 845). The thought they suppress is suggested by
     the fact that Ganymede's name is transformed into our "catamite" via Latin
     catamitus, which derives from the name Ganymedes.

Looking up at the mounting sun

This light of the goddess of the dawn,°
carried on pale wings,
light dear to men,
gazed upon the land as a destructive flame,   850
saw the destruction of its citadel.
The goddess of the dawn, Eos,
kept to her chambers as she saw this.
A husband from this land,
the father of her sons,   855
was carried away in a chariot of stars,
the source of high hope for his native land.
But, for the gods, Troy
holds no more charms.

Third Episode°

*Menelaos has entered the stage from stage left. He is
accompanied by soldiers from the Greek army. The group
stands before the tent on stage.*

Menelaos *Looking up*
This light of the sun is a fair blaze!   860
This is the day I will lay hands on my wife,
[Helen. I am Menelaos, the man who suffered so much hardship.
This is the Greek army.]°
I came to Troy not, as people think, because of a woman,
but to confront the man, who, as a guest in my house,   865
deceived me and stole my wife from my house.
Now, that man has, with the god's help, paid the penalty for his
    crime,
yes, he and his country, which has fallen to Greek arms.
I have come to take away the *Spartan* woman.°

---

847 *the goddess of the dawn*: Eos, who became enamored of the Trojan Tithonos and
    carried him up to heaven in her chariot. In the Homeric *Hymn to Aphrodite*, the
    narrative of Eos and Tithonos follows directly on the narrative of Ganymede and
    Zeus, as here (218-38).

860-1059 The third episode ("Helen"). Euripides gives the director guidance on
    Helen's costume and demeanor in 1022-8.

862-3 These lines seem so obvious and unnecessary that they are deleted or
    bracketed by most editors.

869 *the Spartan woman*: Lakaina (a woman from Lakonia) in Greek. The word is meant
    to be abusive and its edge was especially sharp in Athens in the period of the
    Peloponnesian War.

It gives me no pleasure to pronounce 870
the name of the woman who was once my wife.°
I know that she is in these captive quarters
tallied out along with the other women of Troy.
The fighting men, who suffered such hardship to take her at spear
   point,
have given her to me ... to kill, or, if I do not kill her,
and it is my wish, to take her back with me to Argos. 875
It is my decision not to kill Helen here at Troy;
rather, I will take her by ship to Greek soil
and give her over for execution there
in requital for all my friends who died in Troy.

   Addressing his men

Now, men, go to her quarters 880
and bring her to me; drag her by her bloody henna hair.
When the breezes freshen from the East,
we will take her to Greece.

Hecuba *Looking up*
You, you who bear the weight of the earth and have your seat upon
   the earth,
whoever you are, hard to know and hard to place, 885
Zeus, whether you are the Necessity of Nature or Human
   Intelligence,
you do I call upon. As you travel your silent course,
you lead all things human on the path of Justice.

Menelaos
What is this?° This is a strange new manner of praying to the gods!

Hecuba
Menelaos, you have earned my praise, if you mean to
   kill your wife. 890

---

871 *the name of the woman who was once my wife*: A sign of Menelaos' ambivalence is
   his inability to name his wife at first (if lines 863-4 are to be excluded, as I think
   they should be). He calls Helen his "wife" (*damar*), but "the *Spartan* woman"
   is the description he is more comfortable with (869). By contrast, Helen's first
   word is the imperious "Menelaos" (895). The word *Lakaina* is pronouned by the
   Spartan Menelaos, but in Athens.

889 *What is this?* Menelaos' reaction to Hecuba's prayer, which stands in stark
   contrast to his own address to the Sun (Helios), is understandably one of
   amazement. Hecuba's precedent for her strange invocation to Zeus as the hidden
   guarantor of justice in human affairs is the invocation to Zeus of the chorus of
   Aeschylus' *Agamemnon* (160-83), a play produced in 458; but the alternative
   descriptions of the true nature of Zeus belong to the last half of the fifth century.

But be careful not to look at this woman. Helen is Hell.°
She will make you captive with desire. She turns men's eyes; she
   overturns cities;
she burns men's homes. So powerful are Helen's charms.
I know her, as do you and her other victims.

> *Helen is escorted from her tent on stage. She is flanked by two*
> *Greek soldiers who escort her with great deference. Unlike*
> *Hecuba, Andromache, and the Trojan women, Helen is*
> *elegantly dressed and her hair carefully plaited.*

Helen
Menelaos! This rude treatment announces some
   dreadful thing!   895
Your men have laid hands on me
and have dragged me out here in front of the tent.
I, ... I am nearly certain that you hate me.
But I do want to say something. I want to ask:
what have you and the Greeks decided? Will I live, or die?   900

Menelaos
It was no close decision. The army voted unanimously
to surrender you to me to put to death. I am the man you wronged.

Helen
Am I permitted to respond to this sentence
and say that, if I die, *we* die unjustly?

Menelaos
I have not come to argue with you. I have come to kill you.   905

Hecuba
Menelaos, let her speak so that she will not die without a hearing.
And give us the chance to refute her.
You know nothing of the troubles inside Troy.
Put the sum of these together and the argument will mean her
   death.
She will never be acquitted.   910

Menelaos
We have time, and the time is yours. If she wants to speak,

---

891 *Helen is Hell*: Hecuba is bringing into meaningful association the name Helen
   (*Helene*) and the aorist stem (*hel*-) of the verb *haireo*, "to take, destroy," as had
   Aeschylus in *Agamemnon* 688-90, a pun Robert Browning translated by "Hell on
   men, hell on ships, hell on cities." The same pun on Helen's name is evident in
   line 1214.

she can. But, understand, it is only to hear what you have to say
that I allow her to speak; not for her sake.

Helen
Perhaps, because you believe that I am your enemy,
you will refuse to reply to me, whether you think I speak well or
    badly.   915
But I will reply to you by anticipating the charges°
that you will lodge against me in your speech
[my charges answering yours and yours mine].
First then: I say that when that woman
gave birth to Paris° she produced the beginning of troubles.   920
Second: old Priam° destroyed both Troy and me, when he failed to
    kill the infant,
that bitter dream image of a torch then called Alexander.°
Attend now to how the story unfolds.
This Alexander had to judge a triad of three goddesses.
The bribe of Pallas Athena to Alexander   925
was to grant him the destruction of Greece as commander of the
    Phrygians.
If Paris should choose her over the other goddesses,
Hera promised him Asia and absolute rule over all of Europe.
And Kypris,° who was astounded by my beauty, promised me as a
    reward,
if she outstripped the other goddesses in beauty.   930
Consider how the tale now turns:
Kypris was victorious over the other goddesses,
and this victory is the great good my marriage did for Greece.

---

916 *I will reply to you by anticipating the charges*: The debate between Helen and
    Hecuba is an *agon* (or contest) typical of Euripidean dramaturgy. In this pair of
    set speeches (*rheseis*), the level of language has risen from Hecuba's inarticulate
    groans in the Prologue and Parodos to the cold heights of Athenian judicial
    rhetoric. Similar debates took place in the *Alexandros* and *Palamedes* (Appendix
    1). Helen breaks with judicial procedure in that she speaks first, before the
    accusation against her has been delivered.

919-20 *when that woman gave birth to Paris*: A reference to Hecuba's dream when she
    was pregnant with Paris that she gave birth to a firebrand from which snakes
    flared out. This and Priam's exposure of Paris were set out in the Prologue to the
    first play of this "tetralogy," the *Alexandros* (Appendix 1).

921 *old Priam*: in Greek, the old man. This can, of course, refer to the old herdsman
    who spared the life of Alexander. But an attack on dead Priam is more the likely
    because it is more outrageous.

922 *then called Alexander*: Alexandros, in Greek, means "he who defends," an
    inappropriate name for the son of Priam who was responsible for the Trojan War
    (see the note to 942).

929 *Kypris*: an epithet for Aphrodite.

You are not subject to barbarians; you were not defeated in battle;
   nor did you fall under a tyranny.
All this was Greece's great good fortune. But this was
   the cause   935
of my undoing. I was destroyed by my beauty, and I am blamed
for acts for which I deserve a victor's crown placed upon my head.
You will say that I have not yet stated the obvious:
I stole away from your house in secret.
Paris came to your house accompanied by no mean goddess,°   940
as my avenging demon, call him Alexander, the defender,
if you like, or Paris, the destroyer.°
You craven coward! This is the man you left at home in Sparta,
when you sailed off to Crete. I have made my point.
I will speak next—not of you—but of myself.   945
Tell me: How could I have run away from your house with a
   strange man
and betrayed home and country, were I in my right mind?
Chastise the goddess, not me, and become stronger than Zeus.°
Zeus wields power over all the other gods,
but is the slave of this goddess. There is no reason to blame me.   950
As the tale continues, you might have a plausible charge against me.
You could claim, that once Alexander had died and entered the
   hollows of the earth,
I should have left his house and gone down to the ships of the
   Argives.
At that time my marriage was not compassed by a god.
This is exactly what I tried to do. I have as my witnesses   955

---

940   *no mean goddess*: A clear version of Gorgias' speech *In Praise of Helen* § 6
     (Appendix 2): "If, therefore, responsibility is to be fixed on Tyche and divinity,
     Helen should be acquitted of her infamy."

942   *Paris, the destroyer*: Paris is the name given Priam's son by the shepherds who
     found him exposed on Mt. Ida, perhaps from the fact that he was discovered in
     a pack (*pera*). Of the two names, Alexandros and Paris, Paris is the more sinister.
     It can be connected with the root *pra* of the verb *pertho*, "to sack a city," as
     apparently here. In the *Iliad*, Hector rebukes Paris as *dyspari*, "evil Paris, loveliest
     to look at, deceiver" (3.39; cf. Euripides, *Hecuba* 944). The chorus of Aeschylus'
     Agamemnon call him Paris, "the dreadfully bedded" (713) and add *pamporthe*,
     "sacking all" (714).

948   *become stronger than Zeus*: Euripides has Helen repeat the term *kreisson*, "stronger,
     superior," from Gorgias, *In Praise of Helen* § 6 (Appendix 2). The Greek attitude
     to the strength of the gods is revealed in the symposiastic riddle: " What is the
     strongest thing in the world?" The answer "iron" is obvious, but wrong, since
     the blacksmith Hephaistos bends iron; but then Hephaistos' wife, Aphrodite, can
     subdue her husband.

955-6 *I have as my witnesses the guards*: They cannot corroborate Helen's assertion.
     They are all dead.

the guards° at the city gates and the watchmen on the ramparts.
Time after time they discovered me trying to steal away,
lowering my body from the battlements to the ground with twisted
    sheets.
[As for my new husband, Deiphobos,° the Phrygians were against
    the marriage,
but he took me by force.]   960
Tell me, my husband, why do I deserve to be put to death for this?
You would commit an injustice if you did. My last husband forced
    me to marry him,°
and my life within Troy was a life of bitter servitude,
not the life of a victor. If you wish to be stronger than the gods,
you are living in a fool's paradise.   965

Chorus
Your majesty, come defend your children and your country.
Demolish this woman's specious arguments. She is a bad woman
who speaks well, and this alarms me.

Hecuba
I will first come to the defense of the three goddesses as their ally.
I will demonstrate that there is no justice in what Helen says.   970
I do not believe that Hera and the virgin Pallas could have ever
    been so ignorant.
Why would Hera want to barter her Argos to barbarians?
Why would Athena want to enslave her Athenians to the Phrygians?
These goddesses did not come to Mount Ida for a childish contest
in peacock pride over their rival beauties. What motive
    could Hera,   975
a goddess, have to be so enamored of her beauty?
Did she want to get a husband better than Zeus?
Was Athena hunting for a marriage to one of the gods?
It was Athena, who, in her aversion to marriage,
begged her father for the gift of virginity.   980

---

959 *Deiphobos*: Son of Priam and Hecuba, who married Helen after Paris was killed
     by Philoctetes. In the *Odyssey* (4.274) it is said that he accompanied Helen to
     view the Trojan horse and that, once the Greeks had emerged from the horse, his
     was the first house they attacked (8.517). In the *Alexandros*, Deiphobos entered
     into conflict with Paris, after Paris, still thought to be a herdsman and slave, was
     victorious in an athletic contest (Appendix 1).

962 *My last husband forced me to marry him*: Again, Gorgias comes to Helen's defense:
     "If she was seized by force and was the victim of violence and criminal outrage,
     it is clear that the man who seized her is the guilty party, since he is the guilty
     party, and the party who was carried off as the victim of rape was the unlucky,"
     In Praise of Helen § 7 (Appendix 2).

Do not make fools of the gods° to beautify your ugly vice.
Do not think that you will persuade the wise.
You said that "Kypris"—and this is laughable—
accompanied your son to the house of Menelaos.
As if she could not have remained content in heaven°   985
and dragged you to Ilion along with the settlement of Amyklai.°
My son was a very, very handsome boy,
but it was your own mind that turned into "Kypris" at the sight of
    him.
For mortals all the forms folly takes are "Aphrodite."
The second syllable of her name denotes frenzy and folly.°   990
When you set eyes on my son and were dazzled by his Asiatic dress
and gold, you became frenzied with lust.
And, once you were away from Sparta,
you fancied that the Phrygian capital
flowed with gold and would shower you with luxuries.   995
The halls of Menelaos were not big enough to hold you
and your pampered style of life.
Enough on that point. Now, you claim that my son brought you here
    by violence.
What Spartan ever knew of this act of "violence"?
When did you ever let out a shriek? Young Kastor° and his twin
    brother   1000

---

981   *Do not make fools of the gods*: Hecuba's theology equates divinity with wisdom,
      self-sufficiency, and self-restraint. In her refutation of Helen, she relies on the
      common Greek description of erotic passion (*eros*) as a form of folly (*moria*).

985   *As if she could not have been content in heaven*: That is, could she not act like
      omnipotent Zeus of the *Iliad* (7.17-27), who boasts that, if all the gods joined to take
      hold of a golden rope let down from heaven to earth, they could never dislodge him
      from heaven, but he could hoist them all up to heaven along with the earth and sea?

986   *Amyklai*: A settlement and cult site southeast of Sparta on the Eurotas. It is
      associated with Menelaos in the Catalogue of Ships (*Iliad* 2.584), and in the
      Archaic period was a site of cults for both Menelaos and Helen.

990   *The second syllable of her name denotes frenzy and folly*: Euripides is forcibly
      connecting the name Aphrodite with the word *aphrosyne*, "ignorance," frenzy,"
      "folly." Our word "frenzy" derives from the Greek root *phren*, meaning the
      diaphragm or the seat of intelligence. The alpha in *a-phrosyne* (the "alpha
      privative") negates this. More commonly, Aphrodite's name is connected
      with the foam (*aphros*) from the severed genitals of Ouranos in which she was
      nurtured; see Hesiod *Theogony* 195-7.

1000 *Young Kastor*: Kastor is the only one of the Dioskouroi (like Helen, the offspring
      of Zeus) named in the *Trojan Women* (in 132 where Helen is called a disgrace to
      Kastor). This is the first reference to the metamorphosis into stars (or *asterismos*) of
      Kastor and his immortal twin, Pollux (Polydeukes), as the constellation Gemini.
      Their elevation as stars is a foil to the degradation of their sister, Helen. In the *Iliad*
      (3.236-44), Helen cannot make her brothers out in the army standing before the
      walls of Troy, but the narrator is aware that they were buried in Lakedaimon. Their
      heroization and return to life on alternate days is recognized in *Odyssey* 11.300-4.

were still alive and had not yet ascended to the stars.
But, when you reached Troy with the Argives at your heels,
the struggle and agony began, and men fell to the spear.
Whenever you heard a report that Menelaos here was prevailing,
you were all praise for Menelaos to pain my son   1005
with the thought that he had a serious rival for your love.
But, if the Trojans were fortunate in battle, this fellow here was
    nothing to you.
Your practice was to keep your eye on Fortune
and follow her. Virtue you were never willing to follow.
Your next point: you claim that you stole away   1010
by lowering yourself from the towers with plaited sheets,
that you would not remain in Troy against your will.
Tell me: When were you ever discovered hanging from a rope
or sharpening the blade of a sword?
Any decent woman would have killed herself in her longing for her
    former husband.
Many was the time I said to you: "Daughter, leave Troy.   1015
My sons can find other women to marry.
I will help smuggle you out and I will take you down to the
    Achaean ships.
Put an end to this war between the Greeks and us Trojans."
But you found my good advice a bitter pill.
You lived proud and peevish in Alexander's house.   1020
You wanted the Orientals to prostrate themselves before you.
This was all important to you. And afterwards, you appeared in
    public like this,
beautifully dressed and carefully made up. And you look upon
    the same sky
as your husband. I could spit upon you!
You ought to have come out humble, your eyes to the ground   1025
in the torn garments of a widow, with your hair shorn in the
    Scythian fashion,°
with a becoming modesty to outweigh your past shamelessness,
contrite for all your past errors.
Menelaos, now know how my speech will conclude:
Crown Greece with a wreath of victory!   1030
Be worthy of yourself. Kill this woman! And lay this down as
    a law for other women:
The wife who betrays her husband dies!

1026 *in the Scythian fashion*: the reference is to the habit of Scythian men having their
    heads completely shaven, not close cropped.

Chorus Leader
Yes, Menelaos, prove yourself worthy of your ancestors and of
   your house.
Punish your wife. Do not let Greece call you a uxorious coward.
Even to your enemies you will appear noble.   1035

Menelaos
Hecuba, your argument coincides with my own.
That woman willingly left my house for an adulterer's bed.
And she brought "Kypris" into her speech out of sheer vanity.

    To Helen

You, go face the men who will stone you to death.
By a quick death you will repay the long sufferings of
   the Achaeans.   1040
This will teach you not to shame me!

Helen   *Moving closer but remaining standing*
Menelaos, don't, I beseech you. I fall to your knees.
Do not blame me for a sickness that is sent by the gods. Forgive me.

Hecuba
Do not betray the comrades that woman killed.
I implore you by their deaths and the deaths of my children.   1045

Menelaos
Old woman, enough said. I care nothing for her.
I am ordering my attendants to take her down to the ships ready
   to depart.
She will board ship.

Hecuba
Wait! Do not let her board your ship!

Menelaos   *Derisively*
Why not? Has she put on weight?   1050

Hecuba
Once in love, always a lover, as the proverb has it.

Menelaos
Do you want to give my mind some distance from the object of its
   love?
I will do as you say. It makes sense.
She will not board the same ship as we.
But, when she reaches Argos, this shameless woman   1055

will die a shameful death and teach all of womankind a lesson
  in restraint.
This is no easy lesson. Even so, the fate of this woman will
  instill fear
into their love-crazed hearts,
even if they are more shameless than she.

Chorus

Third Stasimon°
Strophe A

Zeus, is this how you have betrayed to the Achaeans,   1060
your temple in Ilion and its smoking altars?
Zeus, you have betrayed
the flame of offerings
and the smoke of frankincense
that lifts up into the clear blue sky.   1065
You have betrayed the sacred citadel of Troy
and Ida and its meadows of ivy cut by snow-fed streams
and the high limit of the earth°
first struck by the rising sun
and this generous land filled with light and sacred to
  the gods.   1070

1060-1117   Third Stasimon ("Sacred Ilion"): This final choral ode of the play
    continues and develops the theology first announced in Poseidon's speech in
    the Prologue and brilliantly revealed in the "Ganymede Ode" of the second
    stasimon. In this choral song, the captive women of Troy divide the world into
    three levels: the shimmering and remote heights occupied by the gods; the
    underworld; and the middle earth, which is the site of the living humans who
    attempt to reach the indifferent gods on high and their unresponsive dead below.
    In the first strophe and antistrophe, the chorus call upon Zeus and invoke the
    religion of the city and the pious attempts of their city to join heaven and earth
    and assure the safety and prosperity of Troy. In the *Iliad*, Troy is called "sacred"
    (5.648); on its citadel (Pergamos) stood the temples of Athena and Apollo. In the
    Odyssey, Odysseus is identified as a man of many wiles and the sacker of "the
    sacred city of Troy" (1.1-2).
1068 *the high limit of the earth*: It is possible that the chorus are recalling once again
    the relation between the goddess of the dawn, Eos, and Troy (see the note to
    847). It is possible too that the chorus are alluding to the tradition that the light
    of the sun first gathered into the globe of the sun along the ridges of Mt. Ida (as
    we know the tradition from Lucretius, *On the Nature of the Universe* 5.663-5 and
    other sources). What is particularly striking is the contrast between the last line
    of the strophe ("this generous land filled with light", 1070) and the last line of the
    antistrophe ("a fierce rush of fire," 1080).

Antistrophe A

Gone are the god-delighting songs of dancers
ringing throughout the night, gone the night-long festivals,
the golden images of the gods
and the sacred crescent cakes° of the Phrygians,
twelve cakes for the twelve months.   1075
I must ask, Lord, I must know
if, mounted on your high throne in the bright blue of heaven,
you are mindful of this worship.
Have you any thought for this city now destroyed
consumed in a fierce rush of fire.   1080

Strophe B

Husband, my dear husband,
your fate is to wander
unburied, unwashed,
a wraith.
My fate is a sea-borne ship   1085
that, gliding over the sea with darting wings, will carry me
to Argos of the horse pastures,° the land where the great
     stone walls
piled up by the Cyclopes reach the sky.
Here a crowd of children stand at the gates clinging to
     their mothers
weep and moan incessantly.   1090
Mother, mother, *oimoi*
the Achaeans are taking me
away from you, out of your sight
down to a sea-blue ship,
with oars that graze the sea.   1095
I am destined for Greece:
either for sacred Salamis°

1074 *the sacred crescent cakes* (*selanai*): these are crescent-shaped cakes (*popana*) offered
     monthly as the Moon (*Selene*) waxes. They have brought no increase to the
     Trojans.
1087 *Argos of the horse pastures*: This epithet is Homeric, but the "Cyclopean walls"
     of Tiryns and Mycene (both unnamed in this ode) are not. The "walls piled up
     by the Cyclopes [that] reach the sky" (1087-8) are heavenly, just as the citadel of
     Troy was once "sacred" (1065).
1096 *sacred Salamis*: the island already mentioned in the "Salamis Ode" of the second
     stasimon (799-808), where it is closely associated with Athens and the "sacred
     slopes" of the acropolis. It has acquired the epithet that once described Troy.

or the high acropolis on the isthmus° that separates two seas,
where stand the gates to the Land of Pelops.

Antistrophe B

My impossible dream is that a lightning-bolt   1100
from heaven should strike Menelaos' ship
dead center as it moves out
into the open sea of the Aegean,
as he sends me into exile from Ilion,
my eyes full of tears, a slave to Greece.   1105
As I am taken away, Helen departs.
Helen is the daughter of Zeus.
In her hands she holds a golden mirror,
the delight and charm of young women.
Menelaos,—may he never return to the land of Lakedaimon,   1110
to the home and hearth of his fathers,
to the city of Pitana,°
to the goddess of the bronze temple.°
He has captured that ill-wed source of shame
for great Greece,   1115
of bitter suffering eddying
along the currents of the Simois.

> *The chorus has caught sight of Talthybios and his men who
> have returned. They carry the body of Astyanax on the great
> shield of his father.*

io io
The disasters of this land come in a strange procession.
One disaster follows another. Pitiful wives of Trojans,
look on the body of Astyanax brought here before us.   1120
The Danaans have thrown him down from the towers
a grim missile. They have killed him. They now hold him.

1098 *the high acropolis on the isthmus*: Corinth, with its mountain acropolis
  (Acrocorinth) and its two ports on each side of the isthmus. It is mentioned
  as Ephyre in the *Iliad* (6.152), but the Corinthians were not important in the
  Homeric epics. It is an important city in Euripides' world and a power hostile
  to Athens during the Peloponnesian War. Possibly the reference to Acrocorinth,
  known for its temple prostitutes, is a reminder of the fate of some women taken
  as slaves in battle.
1112 *Pitana*: Pitana is a district associated with Sparta but quite unknown to Homer.
1113 *the goddess of the bronze temple*: Athena. The temple to Athena occupied the small
  hill that served as the "acropolis" of Sparta. The statue of Athena is described as
  bronze, and Athena had the cult epithet *chalkoikos*, "Lady of the Bronze House"
  (Pausanias, *Description of Greece* 3.17.2)

Talthybios°
Hecuba, one ship is left to sweep the sea with its oars,
ready to freight the spoils and equipment of the son of Achilles
to the coast of Phthia.   1125
Neoptolemos himself has already set sail.
He received word of some trouble involving Peleus.°
It seems that Akastos, Pelias' son, has driven him from his land.
This is why he left so soon. He could not delay.
He is gone, and Andromache went with him.   1130
She was a tragic sight. I wept as I saw her
setting off from her land, lamenting her country and calling
    out to Hector's tomb.
She asked Neoptolemos to bury this child.
The son of your Hector fell from the walls, and his soul
    broke out from his body.   1135

Pointing to the shield holding the body of Astyanax

She asked him not to take this shield,
the shield that made the Achaeans turn in flight,
this bronze-backed shield, that this boy's father kept about
    his sides,
to the hearth of Peleus or to the chambers she would enter
    as a bride.
[This woman, who is a sorrowful spectacle,]°   1140

1123-1332   Exodos ("Astyanax"): Formally the conclusion of the play begins with
        the words of the chorus at 1118. The play ends as the chorus exit to board the
        Achaean ships (1132). The short episode from the entry of Talthybios to the last
        choral ode of the play might be entitled "Astyanax." It involves Hecuba, who
        remains on stage throughout the play and is the burden of its grief, and the body
        of Astyanax, which is brought on stage on a shield. The small body on the shield
        seems the visual perversion of the injunction of Spartan mothers to their sons as
        they went out to war: "With this [shield], or on it," that is, return with this shield
        or be carried home on it.

1127   *some trouble involving Peleus*: Peleus was the father of Achilles. His home was
        Phthia in Thessaly. He played a role in the saga of Meleager a generation before
        the Trojan War (recounted briefly by Phoinix in *Iliad* 9.524-99). Pelias was king
        of Iolkos in southern Thessaly. The connection between the two men of similar
        names and neighboring kingdoms arises from Peleus' killing of Eurytion during
        the boar hunt in Calydon. Eurytion had previously purified Peleus in Phthia for
        the murder of Peleus' half-brother, Phokos. To escape revenge for the murder
        of the man who had purified him, Peleus went to Iolkos, where he was purified
        by Akastos, the son of Pelias. That Peleus was driven away from Iolkos rather
        than purified seems to be Euripides' own contribution to the myth. Once again,
        Euripides is intimating the violence that awaits the victorious Achaeans on their
        return to Greece.

1140 A line deleted by many editors, including Diggle, since it merely repeats what
        had been said by Talthybios at 1130-1.

wanted him to have her son buried
in this shield and no cedar chest and ring of stones.
She asked us to bring him to you.
She has gone now. The haste of her master
prevented her from burying the child herself.   1145
Once you have dressed this corpse in death's finery,
and we have wrapped him in a fold of earth, we will sail.
Do what you have been ordered to do as quickly as you can.
I have spared you one labor.
As I crossed the Scamander,   1150
I washed the body in its waters and cleansed its bloody wounds.
I am going now. I will dig a grave for the boy.
When we have completed our tasks
—we must be quick—
we will launch our ship and sail home.   1155

> Talthybios exits audience left. Hecuba addresses Talthybios'
> men.

Hecuba
Place this round-rimmed shield of Hector upon the ground.

> Hecuba lowers herself to the ground.

It is a grievous sight that gives me no pleasure.
O Achaeans! Your spears have more heft than your light minds.
Why did you fear this child?
Why did you devise this new form of death?   1160
Were you afraid that one day he would raise up fallen Troy?
When Hector was fortunate in battle, we women were perishing.
Now that Troy has been captured
and the people of Phrygia have been destroyed,
do you actually fear this small babe?   1165
I cannot admire anyone who feels fear, but does not reflect on the
    grounds of his fear.

> Turning to the body of Astyanax

Dearest child, I grieve for the terrible way Death came upon you.
Had you died for your city, having grown to young manhood,
to marriage, to kingship, which makes men equal to the gods,
you would have had a blessed life—

> Looking about her

if any of these things here is blessed.   1170
As it is, you have only seen these blessings.
You have formed an image of them in your mind,

but you never actually experienced any of them in your home.
Poor, unfortunate child! What terrible gashes the walls of your
     ancestors
have inflicted upon your head, those towers built by Loxias.
Your mother would often comb this hair and press it to her lips.   1175
Now your head is shattered and gore grins out from it.
I will not conceal the brutality!
Little hands,° you bear the sweet likeness of your father's hands.
Now you lie before me limp and disjointed.
Sweet lips! Once you had brave words for me.   1180
Your voice is gone. You deceived me. You would embrace me
     and say:
"Mother," you would say, "I will cut a thick lock of hair for you.
I will bring a band of my age-mates to your grave
and address kind words to you."
It is not you who are burying me, but I you, who are
     younger than I,   1185
you a battered corpse. I am an old woman, with no city and no
     children.
oimoi   I remember those greetings and your sweet embrace.
I remember all my care for you, your deep slumber. All is gone.
What epitaph could a poet compose for your grave-stone?°

THE ARGIVES ONCE KILLED THIS CHILD   1190
IN FEAR OF HIM.
                    The epitaph inscribes Greece's shame.
You were heir to none of your father's possessions.
Nonetheless, you will receive this bronze-backed shield as your
     coffin.

          Turning to the shield

You guarded well Hector's stout left arm,
but you have lost your own best and bravest protector.   1195

1178 *Little hands.* In death, Astyanax is monumentalized, as is his father Hector. His
     lifeless hands are the "icons" or images of the hands of his father. Just so, the
     leather strap of Hector's shield bears the impression of the living grip of Hector:
     "Your own sweet impression remains on the grip of your shield" (1195). Even the
     stains of sweat from Hector's brow are seen as his memorials (1196).

1189 *What epitaph could a poet compose for your grave-stone?:* In the *Iliad*, Helen is well
     aware that her life will become the subject of song in future generations (3.357;
     cf. *Odyssey* 8.579). This is true of Astyanax and the fate of the Trojan women.
     This epitaph (and its sequel in 1242-3) is one of the few signatures of an author
     in Greek tragedy. Euripides is referring to himself; the epitaph for Astyanax (in
     iambic trimeters not elegiac verse) is Euripides' own. It is brutal and short.

Hector, your own sweet impression remains on the grip of your
    shield.
Your sweat stained its well-wrought rim,
when, in the thick of battle,
you would lift it to wipe your beard.

> *Handing an embroidered robe to a group of Trojan women on
> the stage platform*

Take this to adorn the broken body of the boy.   1200
Our lesser god gives us nothing of beauty in our misfortunes.
Take this. It is all we have.
That mortal is a fool who takes joy in his prosperity,°
thinking that it will last forever. The highs and lows of our life
are a lunatic, who lurches from place to place.   1205
No man can control his own fortune.

Chorus
Here now are the women carrying a robe
from the plunder of Troy to place upon his body.

Hecuba   *Placing the robe over the body of Astyanax*
Child, the mother of your father places this robe over you and
    this crown,
part of treasures once yours. You were never victorious   1210
over your peers in horse racing or contests of archery,
competitions the Phrygians prize, but not in excess.°
No, Helen, that hellion loathed by the gods,
has murdered you, taken your life from you,
and destroyed your hearth and home.   1215

Chorus
e e These words touch my heart.

1203 *That mortal is a fool who takes joy in his prosperity*; These lines are sententious,
    but they express the mature wisdom of Euripides' *Trojan Women*. At the very
    moment of Greek triumph and conquest, at the moment when the Greeks are
    carrying and leading away the spoils of war, the wheel of all human affairs has
    begun to turn, or—to use Euripides' metaphor—lurch like a lunatic.

1212 *but not in excess*: Anachronistically, Hecuba is making a sharp contrast with
    Greek athletics. The *Iliad* gives us an example of such competitions in the funeral
    games held for Patroklos (*Iliad* 23). The funeral games for the infant Alexander
    (presumed dead) in the *Alexandros* might help motivate Hecuba's qualification
    (Appendix 1). The Greek audience of Euripides' *Trojan Women* was familiar with
    the international competitions at Olympia, Delphi, the Isthmus of Corinth, and
    Nemea. There is also a suggestion of the alternative to the excessive devotion to
    the competition of athletics, a city at peace. The garments that wrap Astyanax' s
    body were embroidered for his wedding.

Astyanax, for me you were once the Great Lord of this city.°

Hecuba
I dress you in the fine robe you should have worn at your wedding,
when you married the noblest of the daughters of the East.
I fit to your body the rich embroidered robe woven by Phrygian
    women.   1220

> *Addressing Hector's shield*

And you, once triumphant mother of many victories,
the shield that was once a part of Hector, receive your victor's crown.
You are not immortal, but you will not die with this body.
You are more precious by far than the arms won by that clever
    coward, Odysseus.°   1225

Antiphonal Lament (Kommos) of Chorus and Hecuba
aiai   aiai   Child, the earth will receive you.
You are the bitter well of our grief and lamentation.
Mother, join us in our bitter song.

Hecuba
                                    aiai

Chorus
You cry for the dead.   1230

Hecuba
                    oimoi

Chorus
Yours is my cry for evil never to be forgotten.

Hecuba   *Bending again over the body of Astyanax and wrapping him in
    winding cloth*
I now heal your wounds with these wrappings—I, a healer who
    suffers,
who am called a healer, but can heal nothing.
Your other needs your father will care for in the Nether World.

1217 *the Great Lord of this city*: A rendering of the name Astyanax, a compound of *asty*
    (city) and *anax* (lord).

1225 *the arms won by that clever coward, Odysseus*: After the death of Achilles, Ajax and
    Odysseus made their claims on the divine arms of Achilles before the Greek
    army. The army awarded the arms and, by implication, the title "best of the
    Achaeans" to the eloquence of Odysseus. In chagrin and a fit of madness Ajax
    attacked the livestock of the Greek camp, taking them for his enemies, and, when
    he realized what he had done, he committed suicide. The *Decision over the Arms*
    was the subject of a lost play of Aeschylus; the suicide of Ajax, the subject of
    Sophocles' *Ajax*.

Chorus
Strike, strike our temples   1235
blow after blow
io moi   moi

Hecuba
Women, you are most dear to me ...

Chorus
Hecuba, speak. What do you want to say to us?

Hecuba *After a silence*
So, so ... the gods never really cared, or, if they cared, they cared
    for my sufferings
and for Troy, a city they picked out for their special hate.   1241
So, we offered them lavish sacrifices of oxen for nothing.°
Yet, had not some god turned our world upside down°
and buried our towers in the earth, we would have been ciphers.
We would never have been the subject of song;
we would never have provided an argument
for the Muse of mortal poets yet to be born.   1245

> *To Talthybios' attendants*

Go now.
Bury this body in this poor trench.
He has all the finery the dead require.
I think the dead pay little heed to lavish grave goods.
These are the hollow ostentation of the living.   1250

Chorus
io io
I lament your mother, whose high hopes for your life
were dashed to pieces.

1242 *So, we offered them lavish sacrifices of oxen for nothing*: Hecuba's final articulation
    of the theology of the play is followed by the collapse of the god-built citadel
    of "sacred Ilion" in smoke and flames. Hecuba's conclusion about the value of
    Trojan piety is supported, and inspired, by a scene from the *Iliad* now familiar.
    There (6.286-312) Hecuba had brought a finely embroidered cloak (*peplos*) to the
    temple of Athena on the citadel of Troy as an offering. Athena lifted her head in a
    gesture of rejection before the suppliant Trojan women.

1243 *had not some god turned our world upside down*: Hecuba reproduces the thought of
    Kassandra, who had earlier attempted to console her mother for the destruction
    of Troy by reflecting that, if the Greeks had never invaded the Troad, Hector's
    fame would have never spread through the world (394-7). The slaughter of
    Astyanax has also become the subject of tragedy (see note to line 1188). Now the
    gods are seen as responsible not only for the destruction of Troy but its survival
    and celebration in Athenian song.

The high station of your ancestors lifted you
to great prosperity,
only to plunge to a dreadful death.   1255
ea ea

    Looking up to the walls of Troy on the stage building

What is this I see?° I see men carrying
blazing torches° cresting over the walls of Troy.
Now some new catastrophe will be added to the tale of Troy.

Talthybios   *To the men who have accompanied him on stage*
Captains, you who have been ordered to set fire to
   Priam's city,   1260
do not stand here with fire flickering in your hands.
Torch the city!
Once we have reduced the city of Ilion to ashes,
we can rejoice as we set sail home from Troy.

    To the Trojan women

As for you, daughters of Trojans, start moving out.   1265
When the generals give the shrill blast of the trumpet,°
go down to the ships of the Achaeans to be taken from this land.

    To Hecuba

And you, old woman, the most unfortunate of all these women,
come along.
These men have been sent by Odysseus.   1270
You are his prize of war and you will be his slave in Ithaka.

Hecuba
Oi' go talaina
This comes as the crown of all my sufferings.
I leave the land of my birth. Troy is now in flames.
Body, legs slow with age, make this effort now.   1275

1256 *What is this I see?* At this point in a Euripidean drama, the audience could expect
    the appearance of a god to resolve the intractable human conflict (as in the
    Antiope) or to tidy up the ugly human situation by reference to a happier future
    (as in the *Hippolytus* and *Bacchae*). But, in this case, there is no *deus ex machina*,
    divine resolution or consoling future. No god appears on the walls of Troy or the
    theologeion of Euripides' theater.

1257-8 *men carrying blazing torches*: The speaker of the Prologue of the *Alexandros*, the
    first play of Euripides' "Trojan Trilogy," must have referred to Hecuba's dream
    that she had given birth to a torch. The prophecy of her dream is now fulfilled.

1266 *When the generals give the shrill blast of the trumpet*: The sound of a trumpet was the
    signal for the departure of the Athenian fleet in summer of 415; Thucydides, *The
    Peloponnesian War* 6.32.1.

Turning to the walls of Troy

I want to say a last farewell to my suffering city.
Troy, Troy, once you held your head so high
among the peoples of the East. Soon you will be stripped of your
    name and fame.
They are putting you to the torch.
They are taking us women from this land as slaves.
io Gods! Gods!   But why should I call upon the gods?   1280
In the past they have not listened when we called upon them.
Now, let us race to the funeral pyre of Troy. It would be a noble
    death
to perish in the flames of my burning land.

Talthybios
Unhappy woman, you are possessed by the demon of your
    suffering.

To his attendants

Take her away. Do not delay. This woman must be taken   1285
as Odysseus' prize and delivered into his hand.

Hecuba   *In a dirge of lamentation*

Strophe

otototoi
Son of Kronos, councilor, begetter, father,
do you witness our sufferings?
The race of Dardanos did not deserve them.   1290

Chorus
Yes, he did witness our sufferings and the great city,
a city no more, has perished,
has perished.

Antistrophe

Hecuba
otototoi
Ilion glitters and its high citadel is ablaze.   1295
Flames lick its walls.

Chorus
Our land has fallen to the spear
and is consumed, as fire lifts up on a freshening wing.
Fire rages through hungry halls.

The enemies' spears are now torches.   1300

Hecuba   *Kneeling on the ground*
io   Earth that nourished my children.

Chorus
e   e

Hecuba   *Beating the earth*
Children! Listen to me! Recognize the voice of your mother!

Chorus
Do you invoke the dead with this shrill cry?

Hecuba
I do. I will settle this worn old body down upon the ground   1305
and strike the earth with both hands.

Chorus
We follow you
and kneel upon the ground
and call upon our tormented husbands beneath the earth.

Hecuba
We are taken away as plunder.   1310

Chorus
Your voice is the voice of our pain.

Hecuba
We bend our heads to enter a slave's quarters.

Chorus
Taken from the land of our birth.

Hecuba
io io   Priam, Priam.
You lie in death unburied, with no kin or friend.
You know nothing of the disaster that has befallen me.

Chorus
He can know nothing. Black Death has closed his eyes,   1315
sacred Death, in unholy butchery.

Antistrophe B

Hecuba
io   Look at the palaces of the gods. Look at our beloved city.

Chorus
e   e   Look! Look!

Hecuba
Your lot is blood-red flame and the point of a spear.

Chorus
Soon, you will collapse to the ground, to our native land. Your name
will be no more.

Hecuba
A cloud of dust and ash lifting up   1320
to the blue of heaven on wings of smoke
will take from me the sight of my home.

Chorus
The very name of our country vanishes into the dark.
Our city slowly crumbles into nothing. Enduring Troy exists no
more.

Hecuba   *A trumpet sounds*
Did you hear it? Did you hear that sound?   1325

Chorus
I heard the crash of the citadel.

Hecuba
A quake, a wave of destruction

Chorus
                                        overwhelming the city.

Hecuba   *Talthybios' attendants now lift her to her feet*
io io
Now, my trembling limbs,
tremble, take me away
Take me away to my life as a slave.   1330

Chorus   *Looking back as they too are led away*
O long suffering city. Suffering, we must move now
to the Achaean ships.

        Exeunt omnes.

APPENDIX ONE

Euripides' "Trojan Tetralogy" of 415:

Alexandros, Palamedes, Trojan Women, Sisyphos

We know of the four plays Euripides entered into competition during the Greater Dionysia of 415 from the early third century author, Aelian. In his *Historical Miscellany* (2.8) he reports:

> During the ninety-first Olympiad, when Exainetos of Akragas was victorious in the foot race, Xenokles and Euripides competed against one another. Xenokles, whoever Xenokles is, won first prize with his *Oedipus, Lykaon, Bacchai,* and satyr play, *Athamas.* Euripides came in second place with his *Alexandros, Palamedes, Trojan Women,* and satyr play, *Sisyphos.* Is it not ludicrous that Xenokles should be victorious and Euripides defeated with plays such as these? We face two possible explanations: either the people responsible for the vote were stupid, ignorant, and incapable of judging properly or they were bribed. Either alternative is bizarre and hardly worthy of Athens.

Alexandros

Of the three lost plays, we have more evidence for the *Alexandros* than the other two. There are the expected quotations in Stobaeus' (John of Stobi's) *Collection of Memorable Sayings* (*Anthologion*). The mythographer, Hyginus, gives us a summary of the myth of the *Alexandros* (*Fabula* 91). We cannot determine if his summary of the tale of the young Alexander reflects the plot of Euripides or another tragedian, but his report provides a scaffolding on which fragments and quotations can be positioned.[1] His narrative runs in the following sequence: 1. Priam had many sons by Hecuba; 2. pregnant with Alexander, Hecuba had a dream vision that she gave birth to a torch

---

1   I cite from the edition of H. J. Rose, *Hygini Fabulae*, (Leiden 1934) 65-66.

from which snakes emerged; 3. Hecuba and Priam consult dream interpretors, who take the dream to be a bad omen for Troy and advise the parents to destroy the infant; 4. Alexander is given to a herdsman to be exposed on Mt. Ida; 5. the herdsman takes pity on the child and raises him as his own son, giving him the name Paris; 7. as he grows into manhood, Paris becomes particularly attached to a bull in his herd; 8. Paris and his fellow herdsmen are ordered by Priam to bring the bull (surely for sacrifice) during the funeral games in honor of Alexander; 9. to save the bull, Paris enters the contests and is victorious over his brothers; 10. in a rage of shame his brother Deiphobos draws a sword against him. Paris takes refuge at the altar of Zeus of the enclosure;[2] his sister reveals to her father, Priam, that Paris is Alexander.

The evidence for the play was laid out by August Nauck in 1889 in the second edition of his *Tragicorum Graecorum Fragmenta*. Since then two papyri have considerably added to our knowledge of (and perplexities concerning) the play. One is from Oxyrhynchus in Egypt (of the second century A. D., a period in which Euripides enjoyed great popularity), *POxy*. 3650. This gives a summary of the plot of the play and is one of several summaries known as "Tales from Euripides." The other papyrus was acquired by Strasbourg and published by Wilhelm Crönert in 1922 (*PStras*. 2341-4, copied before 250 B. C.). It contains lines from a dialogue between the chorus (of Trojan women) and Hecuba in which the chorus attempt to console Hecuba for the death of her infant son, a short messenger's report on the victory of Paris over his brothers; a dispute between Hector and Deiphobos over Hector's equable attitude towards his defeat; and a few lines in which Deiphobos and Hecuba plot the murder of the upstart Paris.[3]

---

2   The altar at which Priam will take refuge when he is slaughtered by
     Neoptolemos. The altar and the slaughter of Priam are mentioned in*Trojan
     Women* 483.

3   The main publication of the new papyrus fragments of the *Alexandros* is that of
     R. A. Coles, *A New Oxyrhynchus Papyrus: The Hypothesis of Euripides' Alexandros*
     (Bulletin of the Institute of Classical Studies, University of London, Supplement
     32), London 1974. Coles offered a translation of the hypothesis. This publication
     followed the monograph of Bruno Snell, *Euripides' Alexandros und andere
     Straßburger Papyri mit Fragmenten griechischer Dichter* (Hermes Einzelschriften 5),
     Berlin 1937. Snell, of course, could make no use of the Oxyrhynchan hypothesis.
     A translation of both the Oxyrhynchan and Strasbourg papyri is given by Denys
     Page, *Select Papyri III: Poetry* (Loeb Classical Library), (Cambridge, Massachusetts
     and London 1970) 54-61. There is also an attempt to set the fragments from the
     Alexandros into a frame by J. O. de G. Hansen, "Reconstruction of Euripides'
     Alexandros," *Hermes* 92 (1964) 171-81. In this presentation of the evidence for
     the *Alexandros*, I have benefited from the edition of the papyrus texts by James
     Diggle, *Tragicorum Graecorum Fragmenta Selecta* (Oxford 1998) 80-84, whose
     numeration I adopt. I am also guided by the reconstruction of the play by Scodel,
     1980: 2-42 (with an outline of the plot on p. 41).

Characters:
Speaker of Prologue
Chorus of Trojan Women and a supplementary chorus
    (parachoregema) of Herdsmen
Hecuba
Priam
Paris
Hector
Deiphobos
A messenger who reports Paris' victories in the games
Herdsman
Perhaps a god (Aphrodite?) who makes a prophecy at the
    end of the play

The fragmentary Oxyrhynchus hypothesis (or plot outline) gives
the following summary (Diggle I):

Hecuba has a dream ... [Priam] gives the child [to a herdsman]
... he brings the infant up and gives Alexander the name
Paris. In her grief over the day [she and Priam gave the child
to be exposed on Mt. Ida] and demanding that he receive
honor, Hecuba laments the infant who had been exposed and
persuades Priam to establish [commemorative] games in his
honor. When twenty years had passed, the boy decided ...
a herdsman by birth ... On account of his arrogant conduct
towards them, his fellow herdsmen tie him up and bring him
before Priam. He makes his defense before the lord ... and his
accusers. He was allowed to participate in the games held
in his honor. [Winning] the footrace and the pentathlon[4] ...,
he enraged the companions of Deiphobos who complained
that they had been defeated by a slave and demanded that
Hecuba put him to death. In a state of frenzy Kassandra
recognized Alexander who had presented himself and she
uttered prophecies concerning the future. Since the man who
had brought him up was present, he was compelled by the
danger to Paris to speak the truth, and Hecuba was prevented
from killing him, despite her wish. Now Hecuba discovered
her son ...

Prologue: Possibly spoken by the Herdsman or Aphrodite,
a goddess who has a close association with Troy both through the

---

4   A contest combining five events: running, the long-jump, wrestling, discus, and
    javelin.

judgment of Paris and her marriage to Anchises.[5] Only the phrase "famous Ilion" survives from the Prologue. It is recorded in the hypotheses, which, like other hypotheses, gives the first line of the play in its plot summary. The epithet recurs in *Trojan Women* 1278 where the "famous name" of Troy is said to vanish.

It has often been thought that the lines from Ennius' *Alexander* (quoted by Cicero in his *On Divination* 1.21.42)[6] come from the Prologue of Euripides' play.[7]

> His mother Hecuba, when pregnant [with Alexander],
>   had a dream vision
> that she gave birth to a burning torch. Following this his
>   father,
> King Priam, shaken himself and fearful because of the
>   dream
> and overwhelmed by anxiety, sacrificed some bleating
>   sheep [to avert the omen].
> Then, seeking peace of mind, he asked for an
>   interpretation
> and implored Apollo to instruct him
> how such great lots of prophecy would fulfill the portent
>   of the dream.
> Then, from his oracle Apollo proclaimed
> with voice divine that Priam should avoid raising
> the son born first after the dream:
> for he meant the destruction of Troy; the ruin of its
>   citadel.

Parodos: The Strasbourg papyrus preserves a scene in which the chorus attempt to console Hecuba, perhaps by reminding her that she has many other sons (Diggle II).

> **[Hecuba]:**   But I am lamenting, because the baby ...
> **[Chorus]:**   Poor, suffering Priam ...

---

5   If the Prologue is spoken by the Herdsman, the only human actor except Kassandra who can know who Paris is, it is odd that in the Hypothesis he is said to be *forced* to tell a truth he must already have revealed to the audience. The hypothesis makes it clear that Kassandra enters the scene only after the Prologue had been delivered.

6   This is fr. XVIII of Ennius' *Alexander*, edited by H. D. Jocelyn in *The Tragedies of Ennius* (Cambridge Classical Texts and Commentaries 10), (Cambridge 1967) 77-78.

7   Snell fr. 1. Snell tentatively identifies the speaker as Kassandra, an identification the Oxyrhynchus hypothesis rules out; see Scodel, 1980: 22-4, who favors the Herdsman.

[Hecuba]:   As we have learned from our sufferings ...
[Chorus]:   [There is no need for you] to groan over old
            evils by shedding new tears.

Five fragmentary lines continue the dialogue of chorus and
Hecuba.

[Chorus]:   Now I see your daughter, Kassandra,
            coming from the god's chambers.

Two couplets of consolation preserved in Stobaeus (4.49.8 and
4.47, frs. 44 and 46 Nauck²) and the single line cited in 4.41.33 (fr.
45 Nauck²) seem to belong to the exchange between Priam (or the
chorus) and Hecuba.[8]

[A] **[Priam** or **Chorus]**:   I know. But grief must be
            mastered with the passage of time.

[B] **[Hecuba?]**:   It must. But it is easier to speak these
            words than it is to bear evils.
Stobaeus 4.49.8; fr. 44 Nauck²

[A]   So, no man is happy in all his life.
Stobaeus 4.41.33; fr. 46 Nauck²

[Priam to Hecuba?]:   Death is the common lot of all. But
            wisdom
   makes it its practice to bear this common pain with
            moderation.
Stobaeus 4.47; fr. 46 Nauck²

The **agon**   It appears from the Oxyrhynchan hypothesis that the
agon between Deiphobos and Paris occured before Paris entered the
games as a contestant.[9] Deiphobos angrily accuses Paris before Priam
of being ineligible to compete in the memorial games because he is a
slave. A number of Stobaeus' excerpts *On Masters and Slaves* (4.19) are
taken from the *agon* scene of the *Alexandros* and explicitly attributed to
the play. I cautiously attempt to identify the speakers in this debate.

---

8   Nauck used Meineke's edition of Stobaeus' *Anthology*. I use the numbering of
    Wachsmuth and Hense, *Ioannis Stobaei Anthologium*, 4 volumes, Berlin 1888-1923
    (reprint Berlin 1958).
9   See Coles, 1974: 14

[Deiphobos]:
> You are a wise man Priam. Even so, let me tell you:
> There is no greater burden for a household or a viler
>   possession
> than a slave who is more intelligent than he need be.
> Stobaeus 4.19.14 (fr. 48 Nauck²; fr. 32 Snell)

> It is no good thing
> to possess slaves who are better than their masters
> Stobaeus 4.19.20 (fr. 51 Nauck²; fr. 28 Snell)

> Test [what I say]. The entire race of slaves is as evil,
>   as I claim.
> All belly,[10] never keeping an eye on the future.
> Stobaeus 4.19.15 (fr. 49 Nauck²; fr. 27 Snell)

Paris responds to the accusation his fellow herdsmen have made against him before Priam.

[Paris]:
> All slaves who are friendly to the master race
> wage a fierce war against those who resemble them.
> Stobaeus 4.19.16 (fr. 50 Nauck²; fr. 27 Snell)

> My lord. Slander is a terrible evil for mankind.
> Because of his lack of eloquence, the captive
> who speaks justly fares worse than the fine speaker.
> Stobaeus 3.42.3 (fr. 56 Nauck²)

> For mankind wealth is a bad instructor in virtue,
> as is excessive luxury.
> Poverty is a hard thing; nonetheless
> it brings its children up the more hardy to bear toil
>   and more active.
> Stobaeus 4.33.1 (fr. 54 Nauck²)

> Wealth is unjust. It does much awry.
> Stobaeus 4.31C.71 (fr. 55 Nauck²; fr. 37 Snell)

[Priam]:
> But Time will reveal you. I will use Time to decide
> whether I will know you as a good man or base.
> fr. 60 Nauck²; fr. 39 Snell

---

10   Likely a reflection of the Muses' abuse of the shepherd Hesiod in *Theogony* 26.

[**Chorus** of Trojan women]:
> Should we praise the nobility of humans.
> our praise is superfluous.
> In the past, long ago, when first we are born,
> the Earth that gave us birth distinguished one mortal
> from another.
> Deep within, the Earth tutored all to bear a similar
> form.
> We possess nothing exclusively for ourselves.
> The noble and the base derive from a single source.
> It is Time that by force of custom creates the very
> arrogance of pride.
> Prudence is [true] nobility, and intelligence is the
> gift of god,
> not wealth.
> Stobaeus 4.29A.2; fr. 52 Nauck[2]

> My Lord, you are unfortunate in what should bring
> you victory;
> and fortunate where you should meet defeat.
> You prevail over your slaves, but not over free men.
> Stobaeus 3.4.31; fr. 47 Nauck[2]

Fifteen very fragmentary lines from the Strasbourg papyrus preserve the report from a messenger to the chorus of the young herdsman's victory in the memorial games for Alexander (Diggle III, lines 5-9):

> [**Messenger**]: being naturally stronger ...
> [**Chorus**]: Tell me, are they crowning him ... ?
> [**Messenger**]: And they say that he deserves [the honor].
> [**Chorus**]: So exceptionally handsome ...
> [**Messenger**]: [He does] all that [a well born man] must [do].

Only another line (13) is clearly intelligible:

> Priam is staging [the games] ...

The Strasbourg papyrus preserves some of Hector's responses to Deiphobos' bitter accusations that he is taking his defeat too calmly (lines 2-10).

[**Chorus** *to Priam*]:   [I see] Hector returning from the
                         test of strength
and his brother, [Deiphobos], your two sons.
They have come to the point of a contest of words.

[**Deiphobos**]:   The man who is difficult when he [is
                         taken] by misfortune,
but then softens his anger is no one I can admire.

[**Hector**]:   And I cannot admire the man who has only
                         petty reasons
to complain, but thinks they are serious and has
                         joined [with others] out of fear.

[**Deiphobos**]:   Tell me, Hector, my brother. How can
                         you feel no smart
when you have been robbed of your prize by a man
                         [who is a slave]?

Ten very partial lines continue the debate.

The only other important evidence for the rest of the play comes from the Strasbourg papyrus and two lines from Stobaeus. The papyrus preserves a part of the plot of Deiphobos and Hecuba to put Paris out of the way (Diggle IV):

[**Hecuba**]:   [We cannot permit] the Phrygians to admire
                         that man, being what he is,
and allow the House of Priam [be deprived] of the
                         pride of victory.

[**Deiphobos**]:   How then [shall these affairs] change for
                         the better?

[**Hecuba**]:   [Is it not clear] that he must die [by this]
                         hand?

[**Deiphobos**]:   He will not enter the Halls of Hades
                         unscathed.

[**Hecuba**]:   Where could he be now, wearing the crown
                         of the victor?

[**Deiphobos**]:   He fills all Troy with his boasts.

[**Hecuba**]:   [Let him come here] so he can fall into the
                         net.

[**Paris** *might be caught in the net*]:
> *Oimoi!* I will be put to death because of my superior
> intellect.
> For other men this is their safety.
Stobaeus 38.20

Two lines from Strabo are sometimes given to Kassandra. They could describe Paris or Helen:[11]

> For Zeus, desiring this to prove an evil for the Trojans,
> and a pain for Greece, contrived these things.

Palamedes

Much less of the *Palamedes* survives. Little significant his been added to Nauck's *Tragicorum Graecorum Fragmenta,* where thirteen citations are reproduced (frs. 578-90). One of these (582) is not a true citation but the reconstruction of the lost original from the parody of Aristophanes in *Frogs* 1446-8. There are two citations from the chorus of the play (frs. 586-7) and two citations of the lyric lament, perhaps of Palamedes' brother Oiax, when he discovers that Palamedes has been executed by the Greek army. Most of the quotations from the play (frs. 578, 580, 581, 583, and 584) are from its spoken parts and excerpted by Stobaeus, who had a special fondness for the sententious passages in Euripides.[12]

Here I present what I take to be lines from the speech in which Odysseus accuses Palamedes of treasonable correspondence with King Priam and Palamedes' defense. We derive four lines of the chorus from Strabo's discussion of the cult of the Phrygian Great Mother goddess and its similarities with the cult of Dionysos in Greece (*Geography* 10.3.13, pp. 469-470 Casaubon). The last citation I translate is the lyric lament (most probably of Oiax, who arrived in Troy only after his brother's execution). In antiquity it was the best remembered passage in the play. It is cited by Diogenes Laertius, who claims that Euripides wrote these lines to protest the execution of Socrates (*Lives of the Philosophers,* 2.44). This is impossible: Euripides died in 406; Socrates was executed in summer of 399. The lines are also cited in Flavius Philostratus' *Heroicus* (34.7). They are in fact appropriate as a protest of the conviction of any Greek intellectual by an ignorant

---

11   For the problems of attributing fr. 45 Snell (from Strabo, *Geography* 4.1.7 p. 183 Casaubon), see Scodel, 1980: 39-40.

12   Scodel has produced the most ambitious and convincing reconstruction of the play, 1980: 43-63 (with an outline on p. 61); Sutton, 1997, argues that Euripides had the fate of Protagoras in mind when he composed *Palamedes.*

popular jury: Palamedes (who is recalled by Socrates in the apologies both Plato and Xenophon wrote for him),[13] Socrates, or Protagoras, who was, it is claimed, expelled from Athens for impiety and died in a shipwreck on his way to Sicily to escape Athens.[14]

Characters:
Odysseus (who might deliver the Prologue)
A chorus of Greek soldiers
Palamedes
A soldier of Odysseus
Agamemnon who acts as judge of Odysseus' accusations
     against Palamedes
A messenger who reports Palamedes' death
Oiax, the brother of Palamedes

Chorus:
Thysa, daughter of Dionysos,
who on the high slopes of Ida
takes joy with his beloved mother
in the bacchant sound of drums.
Strabo, *Geography* 10.13.3, p. 470 Casaubon; fr. 586
     Nauck[2]

The agon
[Odysseus]:
Agamemnon, the fortunes of all men wear different
     faces,
but everything leads to a single conclusion.
All men, those who are devoted to the Muses[15]
and those who live apart from them, strive for
     possessions.
Wisest is the man who possesses most.
Stobaeus 91.24; fr. 580 Nauck[2]

---

13   Socrates introduces the parallel of the unjust condemnation of Palamedes
     and Ajax in Plato, *Apology* 41A and Socrates recalls the case of Palamedes in
     Xenophon, *Memorabilia* 4.2.33.

14   The charge of impiety (and the burning of Protagoras' books) is mentioned by
     Diogenes Laertius in 9.52; the shipwreck in 9.55. In this same passage Diogenes
     notes Euripides' covert allusion to the fate of Protagoras in his *Ixion*, p. 490
     Nauck[2].

15   A clear reference to Palamedes, who is lamented as the nightingale of the Muses
     by Oiax, and who, by the invention of writing, is connected with the Muses,
     whose name derives from the Greek word for memory (*Mousai* from the root
     **mna*). In its entry Palamedes the Suda (P 44 Adler) records him as an epic poet
     whose poetry was destroyed by the descendants of Agamemnon; Philostratus
     has him dream of his inventions in the Home of the Muses, *Heroicus* 33.11.

[Palamedes]:

> I am the sole person to discover and establish a drug
> against forgetfulness, combining consonants and
>   vowels into syllables.
> I made the discovery that enabled humans to
>   recognize letters.
> This made it possible for them, while staying in their
>   homes,
> to have precise knowledge of things abroad over the
>   wide expanse
> of the sea and all that lies distant from them.
> Thus, when a man dies, he can employ writing to
>   state
> the number of his possessions for his children,
> and they can receive the message and learn the sum.
> An inscribed tablet can clarify matters that among
>   mankind
> lead to evil disputes. It will allow no falsehood.[16]

Stobaeus 81.7; fr. 578 Nauck[2]

[Chorus]:

> Happy is the man who possesses
> the art of inquiry,
> who harms none of his fellow citizens
> and engages in no unjust acts,
> but keeps his eyes fixed on the unaging
> order of immortal Nature,
> how it arose, and when.
> People such as this
> are never the companions of shameful acts.

Fr. 910 Nauck[2]

[Oiax]:

> Danaans, you have killed,
> you have killed, the wisest nightingale of the Muses,
> who has caused you no pain.

Diogenes Laertius, *Lives of the Philosophers* 2.44;
Philostratus, *Heroicus* 34.7

---

16   The letter to Priam Odysseus forges in the name of Palamedes proves this
     claim false. But Oiax's writing on oar blades to convey the news of Palamedes'
     execution to their father, Nauplios, was in fact the means of communication
     "over the wide expanse of the sea."

Fr. 587 Nauck² (from the dictionary of Julius Pollux, *Omonasticon* 10.145) comes from a passage describing an oar bound with gold. This might be a reference to Oiax's strategem of sending written messages on oar-blades adrift across the Aegean to tell his father Nauplios of the execution of his son. Nauplios' revenge was to attract the returning ships of the Greeks onto the Kapherean rocks of the southern promontory of Euboea by lighting beacon fires; see *Trojan Women* 82-5.

The Trojan Women is the only play preserved from this tetralogy.

Sisyphos

This is the fourth play of the tetralogy of 415. Like almost all satyr plays, with the exception of Euripides' *Cyclops* (and the *Alcestis*, which came fourth in its competition in the place of a satyr play), little remains of it. Its myth is known from Probus' comments on two lines from Virgil's *Georgics* (3.267-8). There survives a fragmentary hypothesis from Oxyrhynchus where satyrs are mentioned. Hermes is named and the name of Herakles restored (in line 92). The papyrus is published by Colin Austin in *Nova Fragmenta Euripidea in Papyris Reperta* (Kleine Texte für Vorlesungen und Übungen 187) (Berlin 1968) 93.

Sisyphos had a connection with Odysseus. In both Aeschylus and Sophocles, Odysseus is said to be the son of Sisyphos, not Laertes. In this post-Homeric legend, Odysseus' mother, Antikleia, was made pregnant by Sisyphos, the wiley king of Corinth; cf. fr. 175 of Aeschylus, *Contest over the Arms*[17] and Sophocles, *Philoctetes* 417, as well as his *Ajax* 190, where Odysseus is abused for being the son of *Sisyphos*. This connection and the agon or contest from which our main citation comes connects this last play of the tetralogy with the *Palamedes* and *Trojan Women*, as Scodel has shown, 1980: 122-37.

The longest citation from the play (42 lines) comes from Sextus Empiricus' treatment of atheism in his refutation of the dogmatic natural philosophers (*Against the Philosophers of Nature*, 9.54). Sextus attributes this explanation of how humans came to believe in the gods as guarantors of justice on earth to Kritias, an associate of Socrates and one of the thirty "tyrants" of 404/3. Sextus does not give us a context for this speech or identify its speaker. An historian of Greek philosophy who goes under the name Aetius attributes some of the lines we find in Sextus not to Kritias but to Euripides.[18] Albrecht

17 See Hugh Loyd-Jones' Appendix to H. W. Smyth, *Aeschylus II* (Loeb Classical Library), (Cambridge, Massachusetts and London 1971) fr. 90 (p. 439).

18 His citations can be found in Hermann Diels, *Doxographi Graeci* (fourth edition, Berlin 1879, reprint Berlin 1965) 1.6.7 and 1.7.2 (pp. 294 and 298).

Diehle made a powerful case for Euripidean authorship, "Das Satyrspiel 'Sisyphos'," *Hermes* 105 (1977) 28-41; Charles Kahn, who accepts the attribution, as do I, sets this theology in its fifth century context, "Greek Religion and Philosophy in the Sisyphus Fragment," *Phronesis* 42 (1997) 247-62, as do Scodel, 1980, and Sutton, 1997. There is also the explicit attribution to Euripides in a two line citation from the *Sisyphos* the Suda (under the verb χα ρω (which in the imperative *chaire* can mean "greetings"), χ 174 Adler), which I take to be Sisyphos' greeting to Odysseus, perhaps as they encounter each other in the Underworld. (Odysseus sighted both Sisyphos and Herakles when he descended into the Underworld, Homer, *Odyssey* 11.601-26).[19]

The problem facing editors is that a satyr play entitled *Sisyphos* is also attributed to Euripides. In the now standard edition of the satyr play, fragments of a *Sysiphos* are assigned to both Euripides and Kritias, *Das Griechische Satyrspiel* (Texte zur Forschungen 72), ed. Ralf Krumreich, Nikolaus Pechstein, and Bernd Seidensticker (Darmstadt 1999) 442-8 (Euripides) and 553-61 (Kritias). Pechstein, the editor of the *Sysiphos* attributed to both Euripides and Kritias, doubts the attribution to Kritias, but, in a Solomonic decision, divides the testimonia between Euripides and Kritias and tends to think that the fragments of both might belong to Euripides' *Autolykos*, a play in which the arch-tricksters, Autolykos and Sisyphos, are pitted against one another (p. 561). In my view, all the fragments collected under the *Sisyphos* of Euripides and Kritias belong to Euripides' *Sisyphos*.

Beyond providing this translation of the passage from Sextus (based on Diels-Kranz, *Die Fragmente der Vorsokratiker*, sixth edition, Berlin 1952 (reprint Berlin 1960), 88 B 25, I can add three observations. A *Perithoos* is also disputed between Euripides and Kritias, who died three years after Euripides (Diels-Kranz 88 B 18). It too was a satyr play, set in Hades. The language Sextus quotes from Kritias, the "atheist," is awkward in Greek, and I have been unable to disguise this in translation. The forty-two lines must have been spoken by Sisyphos in an elaborate justification of his stealing the mares Herakles had taken from King Diomedes of Thrace and delivered to King Eurystheus of Argos. His defense would be, then, that the gods, as the guarantors of justice on earth, are in reality the prudent fiction of a clever legislator intent on terrifying humankind to submit to his laws. The word *sophos* ("clever," intelligent," "philosophical") bespeaks an important theme of both the *Palamedes* and *Trojan Women*. Like the three tragedies of the tetralogy of 415, this satyr play staged an *agon*. Sisyphos is the

---

19   Aeschylus also wrote two satyr plays centered on Sisyphos: *Sisyphos the Escapee* [from Hades] and *Sisyphos rolling his Rock.*

defendant. Herakles is possibly the litigant; and King Eurystheus, for whom Herakles performed this labor, is likely the judge. He is also the victim of the crime. It has been suggested (by Pechstein, 1998: 447 and others) that the *Sisyphos*, like Euripides' *Perithoos*, was set in the Underworld. How Eurystheus could fit into an infernal plot is not clear.

According to Probus' commentary on Virgil, *Georgics* 3.267, Sisyphos did not get away with his crime. When he gave the mares to his son, Glaukos, Glaukos fed them on human flesh in the region of Potnia in Boeotia. When this food gave out during the funeral games of King Pelias, the mares devoured their new master. (The complex matter of the relation between Neoptolemos' grandfather, Peleus, and Pelias is referred to in *Trojan Women* 1123-8).

The only fragment of dialogue comes from the Suda (χ 174 Adler). The speaker would seem to be Sisyphos flattering Herakles by calling him a better man than his brother, Iphikles:

> I am delighted with you, best of the sons of Alkmene,
> [because you are safe] and have destroyed that
>   abomination.

"That abomination" is Diomedes, King of Thrace, whose man-eating mares Herakles carried away to Eurystheus, after he had allowed them to devour their master. This is a scene from Herakles' canonical eighth labor grimly evoked by Pindar in fr. 169 9-36, William H. Race, *Pindar II* (Loeb Classical Library), (Cambridge, Massachusetts and London) 387-9.

Sisyphos seems to make a defense of his having stolen the man-eating mares from Eurystheus in the speech reported by Sextus, *Against the Philosophers of Nature* (9.54). The defense is prompted by the reluctance of a character in the play to agree that stealing from another will not be avenged by the all-knowing gods. The lines of dialogue are preserved in Oxyrhynchan Papyrus 1176 39 II 8-9 (reproduced with the evidence for Kritias' Sisyphos in *Das Griechische Satyrspiel*, p. 561). Harvey Yunis has plausibly argued that these lines belong to Euripides' *Sisyphos*, "The Debate on the undetected Crime and an undetected Fragment from Euripides' Sisyphos," *Zeitschrift für Pypyrologie und Epigraphik* 75 (1980) 39-46.

> [A] **[Sisyphos?]:** Why are you afraid of others, when
>   these deeds are done secretly?
>
> [B] I fear the gods, who see further than humans can.

The passage from Sextus should follow as a justification for his crime.
Sextus introduces his citation as follows:

> Kritias, one of the thirty tyrants in Athens, seems to belong in
> the rank of the atheists, since he said that the ancient lawgivers
> invented the divine as a kind of observer over human virtue
> and vice in order to prevent a person from secretly wronging
> his neighbor by fear of the gods' punishment. His statement
> runs as follows:

>> There was a time when human life was chaotic,
>> bestial, and the slave of might.
>> At that time, there was no reward for the virtuous
>> nor any punishment for the wicked.
>> 5   Later, in my view, men established laws
>> <for the human race> so that justice would be sovereign
>> and subdue excess, arrogance, and violence.
>> If a person commited a wrong, he was punished.
>> Afterwards, since the laws restrained men
>> 10   from committing open acts of violence,
>> they committed them secretly.
>> In that age, a man who was sage and intelligent
>> discovered in "the gods" the means to terrify mankind
>> in order to instill dread in evil-doers,
>> 15   if they should do or speak or think evil.
>> This is the reason he introduced "divinity"
>> in the shape of a power more than human
>> that thrives with a life imperishable.
>> 20   This power will hear everything that is said among
>>   mortals.
>> He will we able to witness all that is done among them.
>> Even if a man plots some evil in silence,
>> "the gods" will be aware of it. For they possess
>> the power of knowledge. Promulgating all this,
>> 25   he introduced the most salutory of all doctrines,
>> concealing the truth in a false account.
>> The abode of the gods, he pretended,
>> was the region that would most strike awe into humans.
>> This place he realized was the source of terror for
>>   mortals
>> 30   and the source of relief for their lives of suffering.
>> These all come from the vault revolving on high. Here
>>   he observed

the flash of lightning and the dread clap of thunder,
the star spangled expanse of heaven, the exquisite fabric
of Time, that skilled architect. From this region streaks
35   the bright, molten comet.
From this region rain water
descends to earth. He enclosed mankind within these
       dread walls.
In his tale he established "god" [in this region],
40   and by force of laws he put out the fires of lawlessness.

A little further on he adds:

In this way, I think, someone first persuaded men
to believe that there exists a race of "gods."

APPENDIX TWO

Gorgias of Leontini

In Praise of Helen

Translated from Diels-Kranz, *Die Fragmente der Vorsokratiker,* sixth edition, Berlin 1952 (reprint 1960), 82 B 11 (volume 2, pp. 288-94):

(1) The bravery of its men is the crown of a city, beauty, of a body, wisdom, of a soul, of action, virtue and success, and truth, of speech. The opposites of these are disgrace. A man and a woman, a speech and a deed, a city and an action worthy of praise should be honored by praise; but reproach should be applied to what is unworthy [of praise]. For equal are the ignorance and error of blaming what deserves praise and praising what deserves blame.

(2) One and the same speaker [must] both say what is needful and reprove...[1] those who blame Helen, a woman concerning whom the reliability of the poets who have heard of her, the fame of her name, and the memory of her tragedy is homophonous and unanimous. It is my desire to give a demonstration in speech and put an end to her bad reputation and the blame attached to it, to remonstrate before all that those who blame her lie, and to demonstrate the truth and put an end to their ignorance.

(3) That this woman, who is the subject of this speech, was pre-eminent among men and women pre-eminent in birth and lineage is not unclear nor known to [only] a few. For it is clear that her mother was Leda, her father was in truth a god, but was said to be mortal: Tyndareos and Zeus. Of the

---

1   Something has been lost from our manuscripts here.

two, Zeus seemed to be her father, because he actually was; the other was said to be her father, because he seemed to be.

(4) As the daughter of parents such as these, she possessed a beauty equal to that of the gods. Receiving this [beauty], she was not mistaken in possessing it. In the greatest number of men she inspired the most intense desire of passionate love, and with a single body she brought together the bodies of many men who were haughty because of their high achievements. Some of these possessed a great treasure of wealth, others the glory of an ancient lineage, others the glorious ground of their own valor, others, the power of an acquired wisdom. And all of these came [to Sparta], impelled by a passion that pitted them as rivals and a sense of pride that knew no rivalry. (5) Now, who it was, and for what reason, and how he took this object of passion—this Helen—and sailed away [with her] I will not say. To speak to those who know what they are knowledgeable of is measure enough; it brings no pleasure. I have now trespassed beyond the time allowed for that speech past; at present, I will go on to the beginning of future speech, and I will set before you the causes that made reasonable the conveyance of Helen to Troy.

(6) We face a choice. Either she did what she did by the will of the goddess Tyche and the willful plans of the gods and the edicts of Necessity, or she was carried off by force, or persuaded by words, or <taken captive by the passion of love>.[3] Now, if [she left] for the reason first given, he who blames her deserves blame. For no human provision can prevent the vision of a god. It is no law of nature that the stronger and superior is prevented by the weaker.[4] The law commands that the weaker be ruled and led by the stronger and that the stronger lead and the weaker follow. A god is something superior to a human being in force and wisdom and in other respects as well. If, therefore, the responsibility is to be attributed to the goddess Tyche and to the divine, Helen must be acquitted of her ill fame.

---

2   An allusion to the myth of Leda and Zeus as her lover in the assumed form of a swan. I adopt the reading Ώλ χση ("was said to be") rather than the Ώλ γχση ("was disproved") printed in Diels-Kranz.

3   The language missing in our manuscripts can be supplied from the sequel to this argument in § 15.

4   Compare Helen's defense in *Trojan Women* 948-50 and 964-65. The mention of Deiphobos forcing marriage on Helen (948-50) is bracketed by some editors (Wilamowitz and Diggle), but it must figure in her defense.

(7) But if she was carried away by force and criminally compelled and unjustly outraged, it is clear that the man who carried her away is criminal as a rapist, but that the woman who was carried away was the victim of misfortune, since she was the victim of outrage. The stranger who undertook this undertaking, which is barbarian in word, in custom, and in deed is, therefore, worthy of verbal reproach, on the one hand, and, on the other, of suffering the dishonor of law and the penalty of actual deed. How can it be that the woman, who was the victim of violence and the victim deprived of her country and the victim made an orphan to her family, is not more reasonably deserving of pity than words of blame? The man did dreadful things; she suffered dreadful things. Justice calls us to pity her and to despise him.

(8) Now if Speech (*Logos*) was the agent that persuaded her and deceived her soul, it is no difficult matter to defend her against this charge and free her of blame. Speech is a mighty Master; one, who, with the smallest and least apparent body, accomplishes things most divine. For speech has the power to quell fear, remove distress, produce joy, and increase pity. I will show how this is the case. (9) I must show this to my audience by a show of plausibility. All Poetry I opine and define as speech in meter. Those who listen to Poetry are affected by the fright of terror and the pity that brings a flood of tears and a longing that loves grief. And merely because of the fortunes and misfortunes in the affairs and the bodies of others, the soul suffers a private emotion on account of words. Attend now as I move from one argument to another.

(10) Inspired and divine incantations bring on pleasure through words and conduct pains away. When joined with the soul's Imagination, the power of the charm [of words] bewitches the soul, persuades it, and transports it by its witchery. Two arts for witchery and magic have been discovered: these are Misleading the Soul and Deceiving the Imagination. (11) All those, who have persuaded and persuade all those they persuade concerning the objects of their persuasion, persuade by fashioning a false argument. If in all matters all men had memory of things past, and <an awareness>[5] of things present, and foresight of things to come, Speech would not be similar in a like manner [to

---

5   The necessary supplement of Friedrich Blass.

what it is now], for men in their present state find it difficult
to recall the past, to inquire into the present, and to divine
the future. As a result, most men rely on their Imagination
as Councillor to their souls. And this Fancy and Imagination
(*doxa*), since it is slippery and unstable, involves those who
rely on it in a success that in far from certain. (12) †What
reproach, then, prevents Speech from capturing Helen in its
toils and coming to her when she was but a young woman and
carrying her off by [its] force, as if it were a mighty lord?†[6]...
Speech was the agent that persuaded her soul, which it did
persuade, and it compels [her] to believe what was spoken
and to commend what was done as well. Now, the agent that
persuaded is guilty, since it compelled, but the woman who
was persuaded should afford no reason for blame, since she
was compelled by Speech. (13) Persuasion (*Peitho*) approaches
the soul with her speech and can strike whatever impression
upon the soul she will. One can understand this from
the case of what is said concerning the phenomena of the
atmosphere and heavens. These words replace one opinion
by impressing another [upon our souls] and they make what
is incredible and remote from us appear as visible to the
eyes of the Imagination. A second proof are the contests of
Necessity, which are conducted by words. In these a single
speech (*logos*) charms a great crowd and persuades, if it is
written with skill, even if it is not spoken in Truth. Third, the
disputes of philosophical arguments. In these the quickness
of the mind is shown as something that can shift its ground
and create confidence in the Imagination. (14) The power of
the Word possesses an analogy to medicine: its power over
the composition of the soul is like a prescribed drug in its
relation to the constitution of the body. Just so, in the case of
drugs, some remove one set of humors from the body and
others others; some bring disease to an end, others bring life
to an end. Just so, in the case of words, some cause pain, others
cause joy; some cause fear, others inspire their audience with
confidence; others poison and bewitch the soul with a kind
of malign Persuasion.

---

6   The daggers in the text indicate that this passage is somewhat garbled in the
     two mss. that preserve this speech. I have given the likely sense and suggest that
     the poetic word βι τας ("a mighty force") might have been corrupted into (the
     unattested) βιατ ριον. It would, then, describe *logos* as a mighty (and violent)
     lord.

(15) It has been said that, if she was persuaded by Speech (*logos*), she committed no wrong. Now I will go over the fourth accusation in a fourth argument. If the passion of Love (*Eros*)[7] is the agent responsible for all of this, [Helen] will have no difficulty in being acquitted of the blame for the fault that was said to have been incurred. Now what we see does not have the character we would give it, but it is as each individual thing happens to be. In its character too the soul is impressed through its seeing. (16) Now as soon as Vision beholds hostile bodies and an enemy formation arrayed against enemies fully armed in bronze and iron, the one for protection the other for offense, it is thrown into turmoil and disturbs the soul, so that often soldiers are terrified, taking a future danger as a present and actual danger, and flee from the field. Custom has established a powerful habit on account of the panic fear that comes through the eyes. When it comes, this Vision makes soldiers neglect the sense of honor which is distinguished by custom and the good that comes through victory. (17) As soon as they catch sight of terrible things, some people abandon their present prudence in the present time [in its presence]. So does Fear extinguish and drive out Thought. And many become caught up in sufferings that have no cure and in dreadful diseases and incurable madness. This is how Vision engraves in the mind the images of things seen. Many of the things that cause terror are left behind [in the mind], but what is said is similar to those [images of] things that remain [in the mind]. (18) And, in a like manner, painters delight the eyes, when they finish one body and one attitude to perfection, creating it out of many bodies and colors. The making of statues of men and the production of statues of the gods provide the eyes a pleasing sight. So it is that the nature of some things is to please the eyes; of others, to cause them pain. For many men, many objects produce passion and desire for many things and many bodies. (19) If, now, Helen's eyes were pleased by the sight of Alexander's body and transmitted to her soul a desire and the striving of love, what wonder is there in this? If Eros is a god and possesses the divine power of a god, how could one who was weaker thrust him off and defend oneself against him? But if [Eros] is the creation of human thought and the soul's lack of thought,

---

7   Compare Helen's argument in *Trojan Women* 940-42 and Hecuba's refutation in 987-90, a refutation that reflects the argument of § 17 below.

[a reaction like Helen's] should not be a matter for blame; it should be regarded as a misfortune. [Alexander] came, as he came, as a snare of the goddess Tyche, not as the Counsel of Intelligence, and he came, by the necessities of Eros, not the provisions of Art.

(20) How, therefore, should we deem the blame of Helen to be just? Either she was the victim of Passion; or she was persuaded by Speech; or she was carried off by Force; or she was compelled by divine Necessity to do what she did. In any of these cases, she is acquitted of blame.

(21) I have removed by Speech the evil fame that attaches to the woman. I have kept to the condition I laid down at the beginning of this speech. I have attempted to free [Helen] from the injustice of blame and the ignorance of Imagination. I wanted to write this speech: for Helen a praise, for myself to amaze.

Suggestions for Further Reading

Euripides in Context

Thucydides, *The Peloponessian War*, Book V 84-116 (The Melian "Dialogue," 416/415), Books VI-VII (the Sicilian expedition, 415-413 B. C.)

Euripides   *Andromache* (425 B. C.?)
          Hecuba (before 423 B. C.?)
          Helen (412 B. C.)

The Dramatic Festivals of Athens, Theater of Dionysos, Theater Production, Greek Tragedy

Easterling, P. E., ed. *The Cambridge Companion to Greek Tragedy* (Cambridge 1997).

Goldhill, Simon. "The Great Dionysia and Civic Ideology," in John J. Winkler and Froma I. Zeitlin, eds., *Nothing to Do with Dionysos?* (Princeton 1990) 97-129.

Green, J. R. *Theatre in Ancient Greek Society* (London 1994).

---------- and E. W. Handley. *Images of the Greek Theatre* (London 1995).

Pickard-Cambridge, A. W. *Dithyramb, Tragedy, and Comedy*, (Oxford 1927), revised edition (Oxford 1962).

---------- *The Theater of Dionysos in Athens* (Oxford 1946).

---------- *The Dramatic Festivals of Athens, second edition* revised by J. Gould and D. M. Lewis Oxford 1988).

Rehm, Rush. *Greek Tragic Theater* (London and New York 1992).

Taplin, O. P. *Greek Tragedy in Action* (London 1978).

Commentaries on The Trojan Women

Barlow, Shirley A. *Euripides: The Trojan Women* (Warminster, Wiltshire 1986).

Lee, Kevin. *Euripides Troades* (London 1976).

Studies relevant to The Trojan Women

Alexiou, Margaret. *The Ritual Lament in the Greek Tradition* (Cambridge 1974).

Arrowsmith, William. "A Greek Theater of Ideas," *Arion* 2:3 (1963) 32-56.

Burnett, Anne Pippin. "Trojan Women and the Ganymede Ode," *Yale Classical Studies* 25 (1977) 291-316.

Dunn, Frances. "Beginning with the End in Euripides Trojan Women," *Rheinisches Museum für Philologie 136* (1992) 22-35.

Easterling, P. E. "Anachronism in Greek Tragedy," *Journal of Hellenic Studies 105* (1985) 1-10.

Havelock, Eric. "Watching the Trojan Women," in *Euripides*, ed. Erich Segal (Englewood Cliffs, New Jersey 1968) 115-27.

Croally, N. T. *Euripidean Polemic:* The Trojan Women *and the Function of Tragedy* (Cambridge 1994).

Lloyd, Malcolm. "The Helen Scene in Euripides' Trojan Women," *Classical Quarterly* 34 (1984) 303-313.

Murray, Gilbert. *Euripides, Trojan Women* (London 1915).

---------- *Euripides and his Age*, second edition (Oxford 1946).

"Euripides' Tragedies of 415: The Deceitfulness of Life," in *Greek Studies* (Oxford 1946) 128-48.

O'Neill, Eugene, G. "The Prologue of the *Troades* of Euripides," *Transactions of the American Philological Society* 72 (1941) 288-320.

Poole, Adrian. "Total Disaster: Euripides' *The Trojan Women*," *Arion* New Series 13:3 (1976) 275-87.

Rabinowitz, N. S. *Anxiety Veiled: Euripides and the Traffic in Women* (Ithaca and London 1993).

Rehm, Rush. *Marriage to Death: The Conflation of Wedding and Funeral Rituals in Greek Tragedy* (Princeton 1994).

Roisman, Joseph. "Contemporary Allusions in Euripides' Trojan Women," *Studi Italiani di Filologia Classica* 15 (1997) 38-47.

Segal, Charles. *Euripides and the Poetics of Sorrow: Art, Gender, and Commemoration in Alcestis, Hippolytus, and Hecuba* (Durham, North Carolina . London 1993).

Scully, Stephen. *Homer and the Sacred City* (Ithaca, New York 1990).

Van Erp Tallman Kipp, A. Maria. "Euripides and Melos," *Mnemosyne* 40:3-4 (1987) 414-9.

Winnington-Ingram, R. P. "Euripides: Poietes sophos," *Arethusa* 2:2 (1969) 127-42.